Across the Seven Seas

Indian Travellers' Tales from the Past

ANURADHA KUMAR aka Anu Kumar studied at Delhi University where she did a Masters in History, and the XLRI School of Business in Jamshedpur. She has written several books for children and older readers alike, and two of her stories were awarded by the Commonwealth Broadcasting Association in 2004 and 2010. Her most recent books for Hachette India have been *It Takes a Murder* (for adults, 2013) and three titles in the 'What They Did, What They Said' series, featuring Chanakya, Sarojini Naidu and Vivekananda. She lives in Maryland, US, with her husband and daughter, and is pursuing the MFA programme of writing at the Vermont College of Fine Arts.

Across the Seven Seas

Indian Travellers' Tales from the Past

ANURADHA KUMAR

For my parents, Uma and Chinmay Chakrabarty,
my teachers at Delhi University and beyond, and as always,
for Ajay and Devyani

First published in 2015 by Hachette India
(Registered name: Hachette Book Publishing India Pvt. Ltd)
An Hachette UK company
www.hachetteindia.com

SRD

ISBN 978-93-5009-826-4

Hachette Book Publishing India Pvt. Ltd
4th & 5th Floors, Corporate Centre
Plot No. 94, Sector 44, Gurgaon 122003, India

Typeset by Minion Pro 11.5/15.2
Manmohan Kumar, New Delhi

Printed and bound in India
by Manipal Technologies Limited, Manipal

CONTENTS

NOTE: In order to maintain the authenticity and tone of the travellers' accounts, old place names have been retained. The geographical boundaries of many of these places, cities, provinces and regions do not correspond exactly to those of the new place names for them now.

TRAVELLERS IN TIMES PAST

Since time immemorial, people have always travelled. From our part of the world – from South Asia – and since as far back in the past as two millennia ago, people went across the seas to lands to the west and east, and also north across the passes in the Himalayan mountains. Some of these early travellers included traders, scholars and monks. They sailed in their small ships across the Arabian Sea and the Bay of Bengal, and when travelling inland or up north across the Himalayas, they went as part of caravans of camels or yaks.

A few centuries later, around the 6th century CE, kingdoms in south India (the Indian subcontinent – more or less – was referred to as Hindustan then) such as the Pandyan kingdom, and Kalinga and Gaud in east India, sent their navies across the Bay of Bengal to kingdoms and countries such as Cambodia and Vietnam in South-east Asia. These were followed by scholars, artisans and traders.

Scholars, such as Atisa Dipankara who lived in the 10th century CE and others like him, who travelled in the past, worked mainly on religious texts, translating or copying them down laboriously. Traders also kept their accounts. There were also stories eulogizing kings and their exploits, religious texts, and books dealing with law. The common people in towns and villages were entertained by travelling bards and folk singers. Soldiers and sailors travelled, but we do not have their stories. Travelling in the past took time and was arduous; it made writing, for most of history, a complicated business. Many such travellers, especially those in the long-ago past, will stay forever anonymous.

Why were there so few written travel accounts from our part of the world in the past?

For one thing, writing was an activity mainly associated with scholars and traders. Palm leaves that were used for writing, easily deteriorated over time. Paper was first made in China in the 1st century CE, but it was the invention of the printing press by Johannes Gutenberg in Germany in the early 15th century that advanced the cause of books and writing.

Travel accounts, even the ones that survived, were thus rare. In fact, writing about travel became more popular only a few centuries ago. This was because, in times past, people did not write travel accounts as travelling for its own sake wasn't a touristy thing, something done for fun. People travelled only when they had to, or were compelled by circumstances, like traders who travelled for work, scholars who moved in search of and to spread knowledge, and bards who travelled shorter distances mainly to entertain the common people and nobility alike. Travelling had its dangers, and was also unpredictable.

Little was known of the world outside one's region. Mapmaking and its science, called cartography, developed in the west, first in Portugal and Spain, in the 13th century. It went apace with developments in the other sciences that helped navigation.

Ships, however, took a long time to travel across the seas. There was always the danger of gales and storms. On the other hand, too calm seas, when there was no wind for the sails to take advantage of, were also a cause of concern. Ships just stalled in such instances. There was also the threat of pirates, and disease and illness on board.

In this book, we meet travellers from India who, braving risks, travelled across the seas first to Europe and then later, also America and other nations. While we do know of and accounts do exist of travellers who came to South Asia, such as the ancient Greek travellers like Megasthenes and Arrian (in the 4th century BCE and a bit later) and the Buddhist monks such as Fa-Hsien and Xuanzang in the 5th and 7th centuries CE, not much is known about travellers from this part of the world. Their travel stories are relatively more recent – the earliest one mentioned in this book dates from the 1760s – but their experiences remain unusual and interesting. Their curiosity and descriptions bring alive this age –

the early modern period dating from the 18th century onward – when the Industrial Revolution that first began in Britain led to far-reaching and long-lasting developments in technology and science; knowledge in every sphere was expanding, and the countries of the world were learning about places and regions much beyond their own immediate borders.

SAILING SHIPS AHOY!

It was in the 1760s that I'tesamuddin, among the first Indian travellers abroad as an emissary of the Mughal emperor, left Calcutta (now Kolkata) in a four-masted sailing ship. Around the end of the 18th century, clippers, which were ships more sleekly designed to take advantage of the wind, replaced the 'Indiamen' as the earlier heavy sailing vessels were called. But it was the advent and popular use of steam that really revolutionized shipping. Travel time was reduced drastically. For instance, a sailing ship could take at least five to six months to sail from Calcutta to London as some of the early travellers in this book noted. Steamships, however, took only around a month or a bit more. Behramji Malabari, who sailed to Europe in 1890, described the steamship, *The Imperator*, he travelled in. It was like a palace, with over 80 people from captain to cabin boy working in it.

Ships from the coasts of India sailed across the Bay of Bengal if they were sailing from Calcutta or across the Arabian Sea if the port of departure was Bombay. Ships rounded the Cape of Good Hope, which is the southernmost tip of South Africa, then sailed up the Atlantic Ocean, along the coast of west Africa, before reaching south-western Europe and then Britain. They would make frequent stops to fill up on water, food items and also goods of trade, usually at places like Mauritius – an island in the Indian Ocean, the Cape of Good Hope, St. Helena – an island in the mid-Atlantic Ocean, Lisbon in Portugal, and places in France such as Nantes and Calais, before docking in London.

Steel enabled the construction of sturdier and even bigger ships. In 1869, the Suez Canal linked the Mediterranean Sea to the Red Sea, and shortened travel time significantly – ships now took a few weeks or at best a couple of months to reach Britain. The Canal took 10 years to build. Work on it began in 1859 and when it was opened in 1869, ships no longer had to travel down the entire coast of west Africa and round the south before coming up again in the Indian Ocean. By the end of the 19th century, more and more people travelled, so we have more accounts as the decades pass, and some by women too.

Travelling in the past was also a very expensive proposition. People who travelled in some ease and comfort were those who could afford to do so, such as noblemen, government officials or those who had wealthy patrons. Then there were others who travelled on a mission such as Pandita Ramabai and Behramji Malabari, or were serious scholars such as Cornelia Sorabji.

The travellers in this book knew well the risks of a long journey. Compared to the eight or nine hours a flight from Delhi to London now takes, I'tesamuddin's journey from

Calcutta to London took more than four months! No wonder, travellers like him did worry if they would ever return and were constantly homesick as well. There were others like Dean Mahomet who travelled to make a new life for themselves. Others like Ardaseer Cursetjee and his cousins travelled to bring back to India knowledge about news ways to build ships. Toru Dutt travelled with her sister and parents to 'see' the world and became the first Indian writer to write a novel in French.

The intrepid travellers in this book showed an instinctive sense of curiosity and adventure. For them, travelling became a quest to see and observe as much as possible. They brought stories of worlds they had never imagined before alive in their writing. Their accounts remain magical and in many ways, enduring to this day, as they reveal new things about people and places of the time. In that sense, their accounts are historical gems, worth reading for their value and what they say about the world of the time, and about the travellers and their own extraordinary courage.

I

MIRZA SHEIKH I'TESAMUDDIN

THE MUGHAL EMPEROR'S EMISSARY

It was the year 1765. Mirza Sheikh I'tesamuddin, an official in the service of the Mughal emperor Shah Alam II, was chosen by the latter as his ambassador to carry a special letter to King George III of Britain. It was a secret mission, and included a gift of one lakh rupees for the British monarch. However, a few days after embarking on his journey to England, I'tesamuddin realized that Robert Clive, who was then the Governor General of the British East India Company (EIC) had conspired to deceive the Mughal emperor, and I'tesamuddin too.

Clive had purloined the Emperor's letter! Once he had the emperor's promised gift of one lakh rupees, Clive assured I'tesamuddin that he would follow him to England on a different ship. But this never happened: Clive kept the money with himself. I'tesamuddin, however, was very curious about his journey to a land he had never been to before, and soaked in every experience, even those that left him bemused. On his return home, everyone addressed him as the 'Vilayeti Munshi' or the foreign-returned nobleman, and asked him to write about his travels. He then recorded his travel memoirs in a book titled *Shegurfnama-i-Vilayet*, two copies of which are preserved in the British Library in London and the Khuda Bakhsh Library in Bankipur, a district now in Bihar.

THE EMPIRE THAT WAS

By the end of the 1750s, Mughal emperor Shah Alam II was a sorry figure. The Mughal Empire then held little power. Its area of domination stretched only over present-day Delhi and its surrounding areas. The empire had crumbled into several small States. To the east, the EIC had taken control over Bengal and Bihar. The powerful Marathas held sway to the west and south-west of Delhi, and the Nawab of Oudh or Avadh (modern Uttar Pradesh) ruled to the east.

When the British won the battle of Buxar in 1764, defeating the Mughal armies, Shah Alam granted the

East India Company the right to collect revenues or taxes from the provinces of Bengal and Bihar. This was a vital source of income and made the EIC as good as the rulers of the region.

Shortly after this, the EIC army (made up largely of Indian soldiers) fought as an ally of the emperor against the combined forces of the Marathas and the Nawab of Avadh. The battle ended with a peace settlement. It was then that I'tesamuddin, a Persian-language official who worked for the EIC, came to the emperor's attention. Persian was then the official language of the Mughals and also of the early EIC when it began trading operations in India. I'tesamuddin was offered a position with the title of Mirza at the imperial court, which he gratefully accepted. It was still prestigious to work for the Mughal emperor as an aura surrounded the dynasty, even though it was weakening.

I'tesamuddin proved of great support to the troubled Shah Alam. The emperor, constantly threatened on all sides, wanted to use the EIC army to ward away his enemies. It was here that the shrewd Governor General of the EIC in Calcutta, Robert Clive, played his cards well. Clive insisted it was not in his power to place the EIC's army in the service of a foreign court. The British king had to give his permission.

It was agreed that a letter containing the emperor's request would be despatched, together with a gift of 1,00,000 rupees from the emperor to his British counterpart. At the emperor's suggestion that an Indian well-versed in Persian should travel to London to explain the letter's contents to King George III, it was Mirza Sheikh I'tesamuddin who was chosen for the mission. The ship he was to travel on was under the command of one Captain Swinton.

SAILING OFF

In 1765, I'tesamuddin set off on his journey to Britain. It was three weeks later, when they were at sea, that I'tesamuddin learned from Captain Swinton that Clive had kept the emperor's letter with himself, as the purse of money intended to accompany it had not yet arrived from the emperor. As things would turn out, Clive would suppress the letter and later present the money to the king on his own behalf. The reason for such treachery was that Clive felt that it was in the EIC's interest to prevent any direct contact between the British king and the Mughal emperor. He wanted more power for the EIC in India.

I'tesamuddin's *Shegurfnama-i-Vilayet* (or *Excellent Intelligence Concerning Europe: Being the Travels of Mirza Itesa Modeen, in Great Britain and France / translated from the original Persian manuscript into Hindoostanee, with an English version and notes, by James Edward Alexander in 1830*), which he wrote on his return to India tells us of his journey and stay in England. The book begins with a detailed account of how the 'firinghees from the hat-wearing nations' came to Hindustan. By this he meant foreigners, for people from the west usually wore hats. They came to India as merchants, as goods from Bengal, such as silk, satin, muslin and opium, were in great demand.

A BAD BEGINNING

I'tesamuddin set out from Calcutta, travelling down the River Hooghly in a barge. The ship he was to travel in was docked nearer the sea and it took him four days to sail downstream. He soon developed the habit of having a bath in the sea because he had read about its therapeutic properties. As the weather was calm and there was no wind, the ship did not sail for some days. The sailors sang songs and the gentlemen danced with the ladies to while away this idle period, but I'tesamuddin was a worried man. If they were stuck at sea for an indefinite period and the ship did not sail for lack of favourable winds, he feared he would starve to death.

Once they set off, rounding the southern coast of India, their first port of call was Mauritius, a group of islands south-west of Kerala, in the Indian Ocean. I'tesamuddin paid a visit to an officer who held the rank of 'serang', an officer of the lascars or Indian seamen. He also met some lascars from the east coast of India who had settled on the island. They had married slaves once owned by French merchants. I'tesamuddin stayed for 16 days as the ship needed repairs. He wrote that the central part of the island was forested and hilly, and the main town lay to the east. The houses were made of wood and had wheels so they could be lifted higher when the tide came in or there were floods!

THE ISLAND PEOPLE

I'tesamuddin narrated a story that when the Portuguese came, Mauritius was infested by rats, snakes and scorpions, but later French settlers used magic spells that drove these creatures out to sea where they drowned. Then the island was reclaimed for human settlements.

The Mughal emissary heard a tale from the sailors on board about the islands of the Maldives too. According to this story, the people here collected cowries or unusual kinds of shells. At low tide, sailors rowed to certain places on the beach they were familiar with and waited after digging holes in the sand. As the tide drifted in, the cowries collected in these depressions. These were then washed and exchanged in barter at places like Bengal.

As the ship neared the Cape of Good Hope on the southern tip of Africa, he wrote that this area was first ruled by the Dutch, who built the Cape up into a beautiful port city. The Dutch also had slaves – men, women, and children – whom they had purchased from Bengal. I'tesamuddin met some of these slaves, and although they had forgotten their native languages, they still communicated by signs. Sometimes, they would fish for I'tesamuddin, who was touched by their gestures of hospitality.

After a month's voyage, I'tesamuddin's ship arrived at the island of Ascension in the Atlantic Ocean. This isle was largely uninhabited, but sailors visited it often for its famous green sea turtles. On moonlit nights, the seamen hid themselves as the turtles crawled up to the sandy beaches of the island to lay eggs. That's when the sailors would catch them! In the space of one night, I'tesamuddin reported, at least 40 or 50 such turtles were caught. The flesh and eggs of the turtles were much sought after delicacies. Sailors even placed a small quantity of opium in the belly of flying fish. The fish, with the opium in it, was then carefully preserved and fetched high prices as a delicacy in markets in India and other countries.

EUROPEAN SIGHTS

I'tesamuddin's ship moved slowly up the coast of North Africa towards south Europe. The first European town they reached was the French town of Nantes. As they neared the port, the ship fired a gun to announce its arrival. Soon, tradespeople of the city appeared in their small boats around the ship, offering different kinds of fruit, bread and fresh butter for sale.

I'tesamuddin remained in Nantes for a little over two weeks before he left in a smaller ship for Calais, further up north on the French coast. This was a city right by the English Channel. I'tesamuddin wrote that the people here built their homes with stone and plaster, and once the woodwork on the roof had been completed, they placed earthen tiles on it. These houses were unlike the bamboo-roofed houses in eastern India that I'tesamuddin was more familiar with. The common people ate mainly broth, and bread made of barley. They wore clothes made either of thick wool or hemp.

'A MAN OF HINDOOSTAN' IN LONDON

It was summer by the time I'tesamuddin arrived in London. He liked dressing well, and usually wore a *jamah* (long garment) with a turban. He tied a sash round his waist, and carried a dagger in his belt. The English people, who had never before seen a man of Hindustan dressed as he was, found him a great curiosity. They gathered around him in crowds, but I'tesamuddin wrote that he was comforted by their kindness.

One day some people took him to a salon or assembly room of some kind, where there were men and women, and a band playing music. But as soon as I'tesamuddin's entourage – he was still with Captain Swinton and perhaps some others from the ship – reached the place, all the dancing and merrymaking came to a stop. Everyone stared at him instead, and having examined his robe, turban, shawl and other parts of his costume thoroughly, they concluded that it was a dress for performing in. I'tesamuddin tried to explain, but they would not be persuaded. I'tesamuddin, for his part, could not be persuaded to dance.

He soon acquired the reputation of being a great man or nobleman of Bengal, and people came from far and near to visit him. Whenever he walked outside, many would follow him. Others would thrust their heads out of windows to gaze at him in wonder. However, he wrote that some of the children were afraid of him and kept their distance, thinking him to be some kind of devil.

GETTING AROUND LONDON TOWN

London offered a great many things to see. The Tower of London, a strong black-stone structure, housed numerous weapons of war, and cannons made of brass and gunmetal. While there were many brick buildings, he noted that the churches, both old and new, were mainly constructed of stone, such as the immense cathedral of St. Paul's. He wrote about the magnificent view from the cathedral's cupola from where everything – the people, horses and even sheep – seemed reduced to the size of cats.

The stone-paved and straight streets had houses on either side, and were broad enough to let three carriages pass side by side. Pavements ran on either side of the street for those on foot, and horses and other quadrupeds were not permitted here.

House owners had their names engraved on a brass plate placed on the main door while artisans and tradespeople had signs of their occupations painted on a board displayed at the entrance to their shops. A shoemaker put up a picture of a shoe, a baker would show a loaf, and a fruit seller, different kinds of fruit. The owner and his family lived on the first and second floors of the houses; the top floor was occupied by servants, and the ground floor was usually rented out as a shop.

Most of the houses in London had three or more stories. While in Bengal, the rooms were high-ceilinged to keep rooms cool, in Europe ceilings were built low. The floors were wooden, the ceilings generally white, and the walls covered with coloured paper. When the wind blew hard, the walls of the houses shook uncontrollably and I'tesamuddin found this alarming.

ENTERTAINMENT AND MUST-SEE THINGS

In Europe, plays, balls and musicals were staged in a manner entirely different from what he had seen in Hindustan. In Europe a few individuals formed a partnership, or a theatre company. The theatre, I'tesamuddin described, was big enough to accommodate dancing girls, skilful musicians, singers and actors, who performed. It would also hold an audience of around three to four thousand people.

The lower orders, who sat in the theatre above everyone, paid the lowest fare; the middle classes, who occupied the lowest rows, paid a bit more but the 'great folks and noblemen' sat (round) the middle of the house, for the best view. There were separate boxes for nobles and royalty. It was considered ill-mannered to talk during a performance. To express pleasure, I'tesamuddin wrote that the audience instead of saying '*shabash*' or '*wah*' (as they did in Hindustan) beat the floor with their feet, or clapped their hands.

AT A FAMOUS UNIVERSITY TOWN

The university buildings and the ancient churches at Oxford were more than 800 years old but wore no sign of dilapidation. I'tesamuddin had an eye for description and noted how the roofs of the cathedrals were covered with sheets of lead, which prevented rainwater from seeping in and causing damage. The walls were commonly of dark stone. There were old gardens in the midst of these buildings, laid out with trees and flower beds.

The lofty observatory in Oxford had nine storeys, and each storey contained works of astronomy and astrology. In one of the colleges where medicine was taught, there were suspended from the roof, several skeletons bound from head to foot, and used as tools of instruction.

In one of the colleges there were many books in Persian and Arabic. I'tesamuddin read these with ease and pleasure. In a library in one of the many colleges in Oxford, he saw many statues, mostly from Greece, and paintings brought to England from other countries.

A SCOTTISH WINTER

I'tesamuddin travelled to Scotland in winter. On the way, he saw people gliding swiftly along on the ice. He was impressed to learn that in one day, on their skates, they could traverse distances ranging from 'fifty, sixty, or even one hundred *kos*' (a distance used in olden times: 1 *kos* is 2.25 miles or 3.6 km). I'tesamuddin said they passed along at speeds greater than the wind or an arrow, and could be compared to a bird in swift motion.

He described how the skates were worn. On either foot, a wooden sole was attached and affixed to this sole was a piece of steel, usually a foot long and as wide as half a finger. This contraption was strapped on tightly with the help of leather straps. It required considerable skill and practice to learn to use skates correctly, but once the necessary skill was in place, skaters could glide across long stretches of ice with grace and speed.

Scotland had few towns and instead abounded in hills, woods and other desolate spots. It snowed and rained almost all the time. But the people, accustomed as they were to the snow and the cold, bore it cheerfully. I'tesamuddin mentioned the shepherds who slept out in the open, spreading half their cloak on the ground, while covering themselves with the other half. When the snow collected on the cloak, they would jump up, give the cloak a shake, before lying down to rest again.

The Highlanders, as the people of Scotland were called, wore a bonnet and jacket, but not breeches nor high boots. The skirt of their jacket reached to their knees while below the knee, they wore cotton stockings and shoes with buckles. The men carried a double-edged sword at most times.

I'tesamuddin almost starved on his return journey from Scotland to London. He often preferred to cook his own food but found nothing suitable on this journey. By the time he arrived in London, he was nearly fainting. Captain Swinton's servant thought I'tesamuddin had died from exhaustion and hunger. The Captain ordered his servant to bring in rice, a fowl and spices. I'tesamuddin soon showed some signs of revival and then managed to make himself a meal. This was an important aspect of travel then: people, unsure of the customs and ways of other communities and people, preferred to cook what they were used to. The rich would travel with a retinue of servants or else, like I'tesamuddin, do their own cooking. It seems I'tesamuddin managed very well, for by next morning, he had recovered.

KINGS AND BRITISH INSTITUTIONS

The king of England then, George III, was famed for his bravery, wisdom and good intentions. But the king of England was not independent in matters of government, as the great Mughal rulers had once been. In all state affairs the king had to consult his ministers and nobles, and also a few men selected from the traders and the middle classes.

I'tesamuddin talked a bit about the nature of the Englishmen as well. The English, he wrote, avoided self-praise. If someone was praised highly, it was considered appropriate to look bashful, even embarrassed. Flattery too was something that was frowned on.

BACK TO SCHOOL

The higher classes educated their children in a manner totally different from what I'tesamuddin had seen in his own country. In India, he wrote, the teacher was retained almost as a servant in wealthy households. In England, on the other hand, it was usual for people of high rank to send their children, sons as well as daughters, to a distant place for education.

The less affluent people sent their children to be taught

in the town schools. There were separate schools for girls. After the children of the poor acquired some learning, they went to work in different trades; one became a goldsmith, another an ironsmith, a third a shoemaker, and a fourth a tailor and so on. In France and England he described the spacious houses he had seen where orphans, and poor boys and girls, were educated.

Children, from the age of four, were schooled in writing, reading and in acquiring knowledge in various ways. If a man or woman remained unfamiliar with the musical arts, or if he or she showed no inclination or ability to dance or ride, they were regarded as uncouth and were taunted and made fun of. Ladies, I'tesamuddin noted, who could neither dance nor sing would never make a good marriage.

GOING PLACES

I'tesamuddin described journeys by stagecoaches that travelled through night and day and changed horses every 20 miles or so. The coaches stopped at different inns that served breakfast and dinner, and provided hay and corn for the horses too. The post-coach was a large vehicle, in which four persons could travel facing one another. Poor people usually hired horses while those very poor had to walk. The countryside was so well cultivated that there was not a yard of ground on which crops were not raised. I'tesamuddin also mentioned mounted robbers in England, who usually roamed the highways.

ANIMALS, DOMESTICATED AND WILD

I'tesamuddin described the horses of England as being almost as big as two horses of India. The poorer people kept horses for their carts and ploughs, and to carry loads. The English, when they heard that people in India used bullocks for pulling carts or transporting huge loads, were greatly amused.

In England there were neither tigers, wolves, leopards, bears, rock-snakes, serpents, lynxes, nor jackals. At one time, I'tesamuddin wrote, there had been different kinds of carnivorous and troublesome animals that roamed freely in the land, terrifying many people, but brave men had hunted them down, save the cunning foxes!

He remained a week in London before he decided to return home. He had been away from home for two years and nine months.

His visit to Europe earned I'tesamuddin considerable fame. On his return, he was given the nickname 'Vilayeti Munshi' (Vilayet being the Persian word for Britain and Europe). He re-joined the EIC's employment and was involved in the diplomatic negotiations that ended years of warfare with the Marathas. It was sometime after his return that I'tesamuddin began writing his memoirs at the request of his friends.

II

DEAN MAHOMET

SHAMPOOING SURGEON

In the late 1700s, the son of a poor soldier travelled as far as Ireland and England, where he soon became popular as – believe it or not – a 'Shampooing Surgeon'. He went on to open an eatery to cater to colonial Englishmen and even wrote a couple of books: one, on his journey through India to England, where he would settle down, and another on his shampooing technique. The story of the life of Dean Mahomet (or Din Mohammed as it is alternatively spelt) is no less riveting than a thrill-a-minute movie!

THE YOUNG BENEFACTOR

Dean grew up in Patna at a time when the East India Company (EIC) was expanding its sway as the local kingdoms, which had once included the powerful Mughal Empire, grew rapidly weaker. Dean Mahomet's father and his older brother worked for the English Company's army. When he was eleven, he lost his father, who was killed by angry villagers when he went to demand taxes as part of the EIC's army. Some years later, still a teenager, Dean Mahomet also joined the EIC army as a 'camp follower' or a helper to a young Anglo-Irish officer, Godfrey Evan Baker. Baker was only a few years older than Dean Mahomet, who would remain in Baker's service until the latter's death 18 years later.

Baker served in the Bengal Army, one of the divisions of the EIC's army. He rose to become captain and in time assumed independent command of a unit. Dean Mahomet remained with his patron and worked his way up, from 'quartermaster' to a subaltern officer, one of the junior-most ranks in the army.

DAYS IN THE ARMY

Large numbers of Indians entered the EIC's armies as sepoys and also as camp followers. The camp followers and servants, who made up the 'informal' members of army, worked under the 'quartermasters'. They did not fight but helped in the equally important task of setting up and moving the army camp wherever it marched to battle. They transported equipment, managed supplies and in some ways were also like valets to their superior officers. The army was a huge creature, especially when on the move.

Soldiers usually fought till they had made some personal fortune and retired with this to their home countries. In 1783, when Baker retired from the army, Dean Mahomet decided to go with him to Ireland.

FIRST TRAVELS TO DACCA AND CALCUTTA

Baker's plan was to 'see' a bit of India before sailing homeward and so he, with the faithful Dean Mahomet in tow, travelled first to Dacca (present-day Dhaka in Bangladesh) and then Calcutta. They had a vessel with 12 oars for comfortable, smooth travel during the day, a boat to carry the luggage and servants, and one to serve as a kitchen – that is, meals would be cooked on this boat whenever it anchored on an island or by the riverbank.

Their voyage through the delta of the Sunderbans took them through a dense maze of jungles and small islands. Dean Mahomet was impressed by what he saw of Dacca. The city produced fine embroidered fabric in gold, silver and silk. Dacca's cotton cloth, especially the fine striped muslins and calicoes, were superior to anything produced elsewhere in the world. He wrote in detail about the craftsmanship involved in filigree work, in which craftsmen created works of art using thin metal strips. He was also impressed by their skills in embroidery and needlework.

Baker and Mahomet saw the remains of a strong fortress in Dacca. Mahomet wrote that a few years ago a cannon of massive proportions had been placed on its ramparts, but it soon toppled into the river below, taking with it the stone parapet on which it stood. Whenever the Nawab of Dacca desired an outing in the river, he sailed in a most extraordinary barge, extravagantly done up in silver, in which the Nawab rested under a canopy embroidered in gold.

IN THE CITY OF PALACES

They arrived in Calcutta soon after. The city was a great centre of wealth and trade. A man of status was usually accompanied by at least 20 servants, all of whom had different labels and responsibilities. The *bahareas* were employed in carrying his palanquin, there were two footmen called *halcarahs*, then a *consumma* or butler, a *bowberchee* or cook, and a *kizmutgaur* or valet. Some others also had a *hookeburdar* who prepared the hookah, an *offdaur* who cooled the drinking water (after it had been boiled), two or three *sahees* who groomed the horses, a *gusseara* who cut grass for the horses, and then three or four *mussalchees* who served as torchbearers, to light up the path in the dark. More characters added to the numbers of his attendants: There were the *nakeeves* or criers, who cleared the way before them, the *chowkdars* or pages who carried large silver rods in their hands to drive away crowds or to strike fear among those inclined to steal, the *sotiburdars* who carried small silver rods, and then the *piadas* or those who carried letters or papers of importance.

After some months in Calcutta, Dean Mahomet left India with Baker on a Danish ship called the *Christiansborg*. It stopped at Madras (now Chennai) to load cotton goods, then so popular in England. In Madras, the European and the Indian parts were clearly distinct and separate from each other. Mahomet was impressed by the pageantry and pomp of the Governor's procession.

Following a very stormy voyage, the *Christiansborg* finally reached its next port, St. Helena, an island in the south Atlantic, where it gathered new provisions for the voyage ahead. It was already June 1784.

A NEW BEGINNING

A few months later, towards the end of 1784, they arrived in Cork in Ireland. Dean Mahomet, then twenty-five, already knew a bit of English and began to study further. He was assisted financially by Baker. Mahomet wanted to increase his knowledge of English language and literature. During this time, he also helped manage Baker's household.

In 1786, Dean Mahomet eloped with Jane Daly from a family in Cork that owned some land. Godfrey Baker died the same year. Mahomet and Jane soon married in the local church and the marriage (and Dean Mahomet's conversion to Anglicanism) helped enhance Dean Mahomet's social status. In March 1793, he inserted several advertisements in newspapers, asking for subscriptions to publish his book.

This was a common practice at the time for books to be published. A number of Irishmen who had earlier been employed in India and were now wealthy landowners in Ireland became Dean Mahomet's patrons and subscribers. It was to one of them, Colonel William Annesley Bailie, that he dedicated *Travels*. He intended his book, written in English, to serve as a guide for Europeans travelling to India. In it, Dean Mahomet wrote about the cities he had travelled through such as Dacca and Calcutta, the country's geography, flora and animal life. The book also had a glossary of commonly used Persian and Indian terms. The book was recently reprinted with an introduction by the scholar Michael Fisher, a professor at Oberlin College in the USA.

Two years after *Travels* appeared, in 1796, Godfrey Baker's younger brother, Captain William Massey Baker, who like his brother had served as a soldier in India, returned to Cork. William built a fine house, with all the latest conveniences then in fashion. Dean Mahomet had his own house on the estate, and he 'managed' the estate and also his new master's house. It was here, in 1799, that he coincidentally met another Indian traveller, Mirza Abu Taleb, on 7 December. Thirteen years after his return, Abu Taleb wrote a Persian-language account of his travels in Europe, where he noted his meeting with Dean Mahomet.

THE BIG MOVE TO LONDON

Around 1807, Dean Mahomet decided to leave Ireland and head to London. It was the biggest city Mahomet had ever seen yet. Mahomet, Jane and their two small children (they would have five more over the years), set up home in one of the city's growing fashionable centres: Portman Square. Dean Mahomet found work with a rich Scottish nobleman who called himself the Honourable Basil Cochrane. He had returned from India in 1805 as a very wealthy 'nabob' (as Europeans who had amassed great wealth in India were called). Cochrane bought for himself one of the largest houses in Portman Square.

Cochrane claimed to have developed a form of vapour cure, learnt from his days in India. He guaranteed that it ensured complete improvement in health. He set up a vapour bath providing therapy to his clients at his large residence, and this is where Dean Mahomet worked.

One of Dean Mahomet's sons, Horatio, was to write a book on this some years later. In it he said it was Cochrane who had the initial idea of setting up a vapour bath, but it was Dean Mahomet who had 'fitted' up and equipped it appropriately for Cochrane. Soon Dean Mahomet added to Cochrane's bath a unique practice that would become wildly popular in England. This was the 'shampooing' or the therapeutic massage. When he later wrote the story of his own life, embellishing his early life to make things more attractive for his potential readers, Dean Mahomet also claimed that he had been a practitioner of the shampooing technique in England right from 1784 – the very year he had arrived in Cork.

The word 'shampoo' came from the Hindi word *champo*, which meant 'to smear, or massage'. *Champo* itself is said to come from the *champa* flower used to make fragrant hair oil. After Dean Mahomet offered the 'shampoo' in Cochrane's vapour bath, it was soon in huge demand. Many commercial bathhouses, aiming to copy Cochrane, came up soon after and began to include shampooing among the therapies they offered.

However, Dean Mahomet did not receive any acknowledgement from Cochrane for his shampooing innovation. Nor did his rich, influential clients at Cochrane's baths acknowledge this. He was disappointed and went about reinventing himself. He decided to start an eatery to present Indian cuisine to the British aristocracy.

AN 'INDIAN' RESTAURANT

In late 1809, Dean Mahomet set up his 'public eating house', which he called the 'Hindostanee Coffee House' to make it stand out from all the other eating places popular at that time. Everything about it – its ambience, its furnishings, and even the way Mahomet advertised it – was intended to draw in the kind of clientele he wanted: Europeans who had worked and spent several years in India, and who wanted that same experience 'back home'.

The Hindostanee Coffee House was located on Portman Square, quite near where Mahomet lived. Coffee did not feature in it at all. Instead, the menu offered meat and vegetable dishes, suitably spiced and served up with seasoned rice. There were sofas and bamboo chairs to create an 'Indian' setting. On the walls were paintings showing Indians engaged in various activities, and sporting scenes showing Indians. The Coffee House offered a separate smoking room where diners were offered gilded hookahs in which the tobacco, Mahomet claimed, was carefully mixed with Indian herbs.

However, the rents and the eatery's special cuisine catering to those 'familiar' with it in some way, meant that start-up costs exceeded whatever capital Dean Mahomet had. Even bringing in a partner helped little and finally in March 1812 he went bankrupt and closed it down. It meant Dean Mahomet had to move with his family to a boarding house, where rents were lower. He again found employment in a vapour bathhouse.

THE MAGIC OF THE MASSAGE

It was around this time that Brighton in the south of England was growing into a fashionable and sought after seaside destination. Sea bathing was popular as a healthy habit. For those self-conscious about swimming openly in public, 'bathing machines' that were, in fact, carriages drawn by horses, ran along the shore to take the bather directly into the water. Professional 'dippers' waited near these machines to help bathers into shallow seawater.

Once again, Mahomet and his family went about making a new life for themselves in Brighton. Two years after their restaurant shut, in September 1814, they set themselves up as 'bathhouse keepers' on the eastern edge of Brighton.

For his new bathhouse, Dean Mahomet advertised a range of luxuries, such as especially made Indian tooth powder; then something he claimed to have just introduced from India – the celebrated 'culeff' or *kalaf*, which is Persian for 'permanent' red-black hair dye.

Dean Mahomet and his wife also offered clients their own specialized version of the 'therapeutic bath'. This was called 'the Indian Medicated Vapour Bath', promising a different experience with medicinal herbs. Dean Mahomet also offered 'shampooing' with specially made Indian oils.

MASTER OF SHAMPOOING

In their offering of 'Indian' vapour and shampooing they were different from Brighton's other baths. Dean Mahomet began to call himself 'Shampooing Surgeon' in his advertisements. In 1820, he published another book containing a detailed description of the many people he had treated. The book had testimonials from grateful patients in praise of his technique. The book was called *Cases Cured by Sake [Shaikh] Deen Mahomed, Shampooing Surgeon, and Inventor of the Indian Medicated Vapour and Sea-Water Baths* . . . (1820).

His success meant he could invest more into his business. He then built Mahomet's Baths right on the road overlooking the sea, and close to the Royal Pavilion built by King George IV. In the new place, there were separate baths on different floors for ladies and gentlemen. While they waited, clients could read newspapers and journals in beautifully appointed reading rooms. The walls had the usual Indian landscapes again and designs that Dean Mahomet had selected. The ladies had a 'boudoir' (sitting room) and gentlemen their own 'private parlour'. Verandas encompassed the entire building, and there was also a 'sun room' for clients to soak up the sun if they so desired.

The basement had the coal and store cellars, a breakfast room, a room for the manservant, kitchens, pantry, and other offices essential to running a bathhouse. In the steam engine room, the large volume of sea and fresh water used by the establishment was pumped up. However, as they drew in more and more clients, they began to be copied.

Besides his advertisements, Dean Mahomet brought out new editions of his book. It was now called: *Shampooing, or, Benefits Resulting from the Use of The Indian Medicated Vapour Bath, as Introduced into this Country by S.D. Mahomed (A Native of India)*. Between 1822, 1826 and 1838, three editions of his book appeared. He offered a different version of his life story in this book. Dean Mahomet now claimed to have received some kind of medical training in India. He also raised his age by over a decade in the hope that this made him seem more 'respectable'.

In this period, royalty numbered among his clients, including King George IV (who ruled between 1820–30) and King William IV (who ruled between 1830–37). He was even awarded Warrants of Appointment as royal 'Shampooing Surgeon' to Their Majesties.

SOME ROTTEN BAD LUCK

However, Dean Mahomet's success was tragically short-lived. By the late 1830s, Dean Mahomet's connection to the

British royal family faded. King William's successor and niece Queen Victoria, for all of Dean Mahomet's fervent expressions of loyalty, never visited his Baths. She did not really like Brighton much.

By the early 1840s, Dean Mahomet found himself facing a financial breakdown again. He had never managed his money well, investing and borrowing against his capacity. At the time he died in February 1851, two months after his wife Jane, he had been largely forgotten. Two of his grandchildren, however, came to prominence later: One, Frederick Horatio was a reputed surgeon known for his contributions to understanding hypertension (high blood pressure) and another, James, served as a vicar in a town in Sussex County towards the end of the 19th century.

III

MIRZA ABU TALEB KHAN

THE 'PERSIAN PRINCE'

A nobleman and scholar of Persian, Mirza Abu Taleb Khan served first in the kingdom of Avadh and then with the East India Company (EIC). However, Abu Taleb met with some personal misfortune and his career too took a downturn, so he took up the invitation of a Scottish friend, David Richardson, to travel with him to Britain. The account he wrote of his travels was very detailed, descriptive and very amusing. Abu Taleb described the behaviour of different people he met, the experiences he had and the stories he heard.

FRIENDS AND ENEMIES IN AVADH

Unlike Dean Mahomet, Abu Taleb came from an illustrious family that originally belonged to Persia. They moved to India in the early 18th century. This was the time when the once magnificent Mughal Empire was in decline, but the provinces around were more powerful. One of these was Avadh, now eastern Uttar Pradesh, with its capital at Lucknow. It drew a host of talented people, hoping to join the Nawab's service.

Abu Taleb's father became one of the favourite nobles of the then Nawab of Avadh, Abul Munner Khan Safdar Jung. As the Nawab trusted him, Abu Taleb's father joined the service of the Nawab's nephew, the deputy governor of Avadh. But the Nawab died and his son Shuja-ud-Daulah succeeded his father. The new Nawab was suspicious of his cousin and had him killed. Now fearing for his life, Abu Taleb's father fled to Calcutta, where the EIC was steadily growing in power.

Abu Taleb remained in Lucknow with his mother. Some years later, with his mother, Abu Taleb left for Bengal, moving from Lucknow to Patna, and then by boat to Murshidabad, where the Nawab of Bengal had his capital. Abu Taleb was married at the age of 14 to a niece of Muzaffar Jung, then Nawab of Bengal.

After Shuja-ud-Daulah's death, however, his son Asaf-ud-Daulah invited Abu Taleb's family back to Lucknow. Mirza Abu Taleb, for by now he had the title of a scholar ('Mirza'), was appointed a revenue collector at Etah, but he continued to face hurdles in his career, especially from other jealous nobles in Avadh. So he moved to Gorakhpur in the east of Avadh, where the EIC was then stationed, and sought service with the Company. His knowledge of Persian proved an advantage, and he managed to draw the attention of Lord Cornwallis, then Governor General of the East India Company.

Still, this did not end the upheavals in his life. His old friends in Avadh now thought he was a spy for the British, and the latter in turn did use him to keep an eye on intrigues in the rich province of Avadh. Then he lost his four-year-old son to a sudden illness. This was when a friend, David Richardson, a Scotsman, who was ailing, asked Abu Taleb to travel with him to Britain. The latter jumped at the offer. He wrote vividly about his travels on his return to India.

SETTING SAIL

The journey itself began in a nightmarish way. Richardson and Abu Taleb left on 7 February 1799 on a barge from Calcutta. Big ships then could not really sail all the way up the River Ganges to Calcutta. So the barge took them downstream, right at the river mouth at Kedjeree (Khijri) where the bigger vessel was anchored. The first ship they had booked tickets for burnt down, and so they settled for a Danish ship.

This ship too was in extremely bad shape. The Danish captain of the ship then vanished for a fortnight. As they had been the last to board, they were given the worst cabins. In a cabin close by, there was a three-year-old child who bawled constantly, thoroughly irritating Abu Taleb.

They finally departed on 16 February, but the ship encountered several obstacles. The sand beds close to the river mouth were particularly dangerous and could trap ships on the move, especially if these were not navigated skilfully. The ship negotiated this stretch only to be warned of the presence of a French warship cruising close. They were forbidden to move further. Those were the days when England and France were each other's bitterest enemies.

It was only after a few days that an English warship finally managed to capture the French frigate. But the Englishmen lost 25 men in the short battle; the French lost 200 and also their captain. The next day, fifteen small warships with armed soldiers came down the river to escort the prisoners. After all this excitement, Abu Taleb finally set sail.

THE ISLANDS

After some days of uneventful sailing, everyone realized that the captain had changed course. The ship had been moving south, but it had taken a noticeably eastward turn. The captain said water supplies had been depleted due to the long wait as the battle raged, and the ship needed to replenish its water supplies on the Nicobar islands.

Their ship's approach to Car Nicobar, the largest of the islands, was thwarted by winds and only towards midnight was the ship able to drop anchor on one of the smaller islands. As the island came closer into view, the islanders sailed up in their small boats with an abundance of offerings - coconuts, pineapples, lime, plantains, other fruits, and also ducks and fowls - in exchange for cloth, tobacco and cutlery. To Abu Taleb, they looked like inhabitants from Pegu (present-day Myanmar) or China. Their houses were made of wood and bamboo, in a circular manner like corn stacks. They also appeared to be adept boatbuilders and could build boats in the European fashion.

STORMY SEAS

In the tropics, the sun was high. It often rained, but they were sailing during a period of the 'calms'. The absence of wind meant the ship made slow progress. Abu Taleb often noticed large birds flying past the ship. As they sailed on, they encountered the trade winds that were favourable for ship navigation at these latitudes. To entertain the passengers, a pantomime was once enacted on board, with one of the sailors playing Neptune, the ancient Roman sea god. They demanded those who had never crossed 'the line to the west' to offer gifts to the god.

A few days later, in the southern latitudes, they encountered schools of flying fish. These could fly high almost up to five feet and traverse long distances. Seasons, as Abu Taleb was aware, were reversed in the hemispheres. In May, Abu Taleb wrote about how cold he felt. Past the islands of Mauritius and Madagascar in the Indian Ocean, they sailed on, keeping an eye out for French warships for hostilities were still on between Britain and France.

Then a storm broke out and lasted four days. Abu Taleb's neighbour, one Mr Grand, who was in the next cabin and was in the habit of calling out loud at the slightest noise, fell through the thin partition and landed on a sleeping Abu Taleb. It made the latter very indignant.

UNENDING TRAVAILS IN AFRICA

As they approached the coast of South Africa, they sighted whales that came quite close to the ship. Abu Taleb noted how these were four times the size of elephants and threw out mountains of water on the surface with their huge blowholes. They were greatly valued for their oil and their whalebones, but hunting them was a very risky enterprise and demanded the most skilled of sailors.

There was a storm again and the ship's hatches were kept covered at all times. The passengers had to spend time in the dark for even candles were scarce now. They sat like 'dead bodies', as Abu Taleb described. It was June by the time they reached Cape Town.

The hardships he endured on board compelled Abu Taleb to later advise travellers to travel only in English vessels and not those of other countries, for the latter were not as well built as British ships. He advised people to go on voyages only if they had enough wealth to ensure certain provisions for themselves. The water too was sometimes not potable, and fellow passengers could often be most inconsiderate.

Cape Town in South Africa was distinguishable by its twin natural landmarks: the Table Mountain and Sugar Loaf Hill. Abu Taleb wrote that they did resemble the objects they had been named after. At Cape Town, they anchored near False Bay. The British had secured the Cape of Good Hope, with its chief town of Cape Town, from the Dutch only recently, in 1795. Its capture secured the sea routes to India.

Abu Taleb rented a place at a reasonable price but soon found himself being moved to poorer and ill-furnished rooms till the landlord said that the rent he was paying was just not enough. So Abu Taleb resolved to leave the city as soon as he could. Like the others, he was staying put in the hope of the arrival of an English vessel that would take them to London. He had had enough of the Danish vessel and its captain.

One day he decided to make a journey towards Cape Town proper, which took almost a day. The narrow road widened considerably as they neared Cape Town. It was lined with hedges as well. On the way, there were rest houses for travellers. Table Mountain loomed over the city; some houses were built so close to it that Abu Taleb feared the mountain would topple over them. The residents of the city were known to climb the mountain right to the very top for picnics, and Abu Taleb especially admired the grace and skill of the ladies as they took on the steepest slopes.

He finally set sail for Europe in an English ship called the *Britannia*.

STRANGE SEA CREATURES

The first land they sighted was the island of St. Helena right in the middle of the Atlantic Ocean. This remote island would serve as the place of exile for the defeated French emperor Napoleon a decade or so later.

They set sail after a few days. The English-speaking sailors on board regaled him with many interesting stories. Once the ship's captain told him of the time he and a few of his crew had alighted off the coast of Africa. Just as they stopped, several strange water creatures emerged from the sea, resembling something midway between a horse and an ass. They were perhaps seals of some kind. As the creatures returned towards the water, the captain fired and killed one of them. This enraged the animals and they turned on the frightened crew. The sailors managed to evade the creatures only by hiding behind the rocks on shore. It was finally towards sunset that they managed to wade across to where their boats were anchored. However, the strange creatures soon caught up and destroyed one of their boats, forcing all the sailors to crowd into one boat to make a quick and desperate escape.

As Abu Taleb's ship neared the west coast of Europe and towards the English Channel, gale-force winds compelled the captain to turn the ship to the coast of Ireland instead. They finally docked at Cork on the southern tip of the Irish coast, and as Abu Taleb noted, it was 6 December 1799. It was almost 10 months since he had left home.

FINALLY, IRELAND

The town of Cork was built in the shape of a crescent and defended by small forts. A large river flowed into the sea close by. The river, the bay with the fleet of ships anchored in it, the hills, the forts and the city itself with its elegant houses and romantic cottages, made a memorable impression on Abu Taleb.

At the post office, the postmistress turned out to be very helpful and insisted that Abu Taleb and his friends stay for a meal. She prepared it herself, assisted by her children. He was astonished by her generosity and capacity for hard work. She had 21 children, of whom 18 had reached adulthood, and yet she didn't look very old. Abu Taleb recounted the repast in every detail – there was fish, beef, butter, potatoes and the fresh vegetables Cork was famous for and sent to England – as it had indeed been a long time since he had had so sumptuous a meal.

The next morning she provided them with horses to tour the city. Later, they crossed the river Lee in small ferries to reach the part of town that served as the business quarter. Its canals had drawbridges that were raised and lowered whenever a ship appeared.

It was at Cork that Abu Taleb met Captain William Massey Baker at whose house he made the acquaintance of Dean Mahomet. Baker invited him to his imposing residence and Abu Taleb was, in particular, very impressed by the kitchen, which was by far the biggest he had ever seen. During this time Abu Taleb also learnt that Lord Cornwallis, who had once been Governor General of the EIC in India, was in Dublin, Ireland's capital. He decided to travel by road to the city, to meet him and then move on to London.

Abu Taleb and his friend David Richardson, who had been with him all through the journey, set out in a mail coach for Dublin and London. As the roads were not very safe, the coach was escorted by soldiers on horses. They reached Dublin on the third day. He noted that the villages of the countryside resembled those of India. Food and other provisions appeared costlier. As it was also a much colder country than India, people spent more on keeping themselves warm. They mainly subsisted on potatoes, though the countryside cultivated a wide variety of other crops like wheat, barley, peas and turnips.

Abu Taleb wrote of the widespread use of a fuel called 'coal' that he had first read about in a Persian book. It was coal that would propel, along with the use of iron to make steel, the Industrial Revolution in Britain, enabling her to become the world's most powerful nation, a position it held for a century and more. In India, it was wood that was commonly used for fuel, for domestic as well as for small-scale manufacturing purposes such as for metallurgy.

HOW DUBLIN FELT LIKE HOME

Abu Taleb was impressed by the city of Dublin. The streets were lit up at night with candles and it reminded him of the rare occasions in his native Lucknow when the Imambara was lit up during the reign of Nawab Asad-ud-Daulah.

He was always astonished by the crowds of people on the streets, but they hardly dashed against anyone.

He counted as many as 700 registered carriages plying the streets. Nobles and men of high rank had their own carriages drawn by horses. Most of the city squares had a fountain, and the statues adorning the fountains were usually those of a lion or the king on his horse. Whether it was London, Paris or Dublin, there were statues at the entrance to gates and burial grounds and even near the chimneys of houses. On one occasion, Abu Taleb witnessed the sale of a damaged statue in London, which went for an exorbitant amount.

Canals ran through the city of Dublin. Boats that brought in goods were in turn drawn by horses that ran along roads built alongside the canals and shaded by trees. In the library of the college at Dublin, he was impressed by the presence of many Persian books and manuscripts, including some very rare copies of the *Shahnameh*, the classic Persian text written by Firdausi in the 13th century.

Abu Taleb considered the days he spent in Dublin as the most agreeable ones of his life. He attended a play at the public theatre, which dealt with the defeat of Tipu Sultan in the battle of Seringapattinam (1799). Tipu had just been defeated by the British, and Abu Taleb agreed that the account was true in every detail.

The people, he wrote, were very hospitable and never put out by his awkwardness or his ignorance. As with I'tesamuddin, Abu Taleb also wrote that they were very curious about him. Some would hazard a guess that he was a Russian general who had been expected to visit Dublin for some time, still others argued over whether he was a Spanish or a German nobleman.

Abu Taleb wrote of the heavy snowfall that winter. It got very cold and not even three blankets could suffice to keep him warm. Sometimes, to beat the frost, he would walk very fast and for long distances, and that helped.

MIXING WITH LONDON'S HIGH SOCIETY

He set out for London again in a mail coach, stopping at cities like Holyhead on the way. By the time Abu Taleb reached London, it was almost a year since he had left Calcutta.

In London, he met several people in the higher echelons of nobility. He was introduced to the King George IV and Queen Charlotte, who insisted that he attend court. This made him greatly sought after. One of his reasons for coming to London, Abu Taleb wrote, was to seek support to open an academy in London where young men keen on working with the EIC or going out east, could learn languages such as Hindustani, Persian and Arabic. Abu Taleb also hoped to propagate the cause of the Persian language, believing that if one student was taught, he would in turn teach others.

However, the powers that be, the EIC officials and the powerful ministers who had a voice in Indian matters in Britain, dithered over this issue and this distressed Abu Taleb very much. It was only when he had made plans to leave for India that a decision of some sort come through, but by then Abu Taleb had made up his mind to return.

WHAT ENGLAND WAS ALL ABOUT

Abu Taleb made several observations on British institutions. He was impressed and also confused by the British judicial system. He saw something similar in the new systems of civil courts and law that the British were just beginning to introduce in India, though personal matters were still settled by religious authorities in India.

The English, Abu Taleb wrote, were always busy and sometimes pretended to be so. If someone came calling, they would instruct their valets or servants to tell the visitor that the master was very busy. They were also given to some extravagance. Kitchens were chock-a-block with utensils and there was just too much furniture in most houses. The beds were piled with feather mattresses into which one could literally sink. Over these mattresses, sheets and quilts were placed, and all this was tucked into three sides. So one had to crawl into bed from one side, reminding Abu Taleb of a bear climbing into his cave!

The people were highly respectful of institutions. They were also very inventive, and their innovations with steam power that Abu Taleb saw first-hand were to prove immensely useful over the decades. While the city caught fire almost too frequently because many houses were made of wood, they were very adroit in extinguishing these too. Fire machines placed on carriages and drawn by horses could squirt water via pumps across a distance of 50 yards. There were water pipes running under the streets and these supplied water to the fire pipes at convenient locations.

THE HOMEWARD JOURNEY

Abu Taleb took a different route on his way back to India. He travelled via Lyon in France, and then sailed down the Rhone valley to Marseilles in south France, then moved to Genoa in Italy, the island of Malta and on to Constantinople (now Istanbul) in Turkey. Later he made stops in the cities of Basra and Baghdad in present-day Iraq, before returning to India via Persia.

He found the French countryside beautiful. The fields were then ripening with corn, and he noted the vineyards and orchards too. The cows, though, looked poorly nourished 'almost like the ones in Hindustan', he wrote. Paris appeared to be an extensive and noble city, superior to London in many ways. Its public buildings were all made of stone and most were over eight storeys high. The river Seine ran through the city and had canals cut into it. Various kinds of boats plied these canals and some of these were elaborately done up, even offering hot and cold baths depending on the season.

The Palais Royal in Paris was a popular place to visit. The pleasure gardens or the Tuileries also drew many visitors. The Louvre Museum was stocked with marvellous pieces of art and sculpture curated from all over the world. At Lyons, famous for its dyeing industry, Abu Taleb had his turban dyed a fascinating purple.

On his way to Constantinople from France, he stopped at Genoa. As they docked at the bay of Genoa, a health boat came up for inspection. The dreaded plague had just broken out, and if anything infected was found or someone was sick on board, the ship was quarantined for 40 days.

However, they got an all-clear, and Abu Taleb travelled to Leghorn in Tuscany where he found an unusual water shortage. People queued up at fountains for hours to fill up their vessels with water. As he rested, a man attempted to make off with his turban. When he raised an alarm, the thief simply ripped the turban in half and made off with it!

As he moved towards Europe, Abu Taleb made observations on the many kingdoms that made up the continent. There were several small kingdoms, but Russia was the most powerful of them all. Some of the kings were despots. The five most powerful kings of Europe at the time were those of Russia, Prussia, England, France and Spain. He wrote of the events that led up to the French Revolution of 1789. King Louis XVI had been adamant about not ceding power to the parliament and had to pay for it with his life. The king's execution alarmed the rulers of other European countries. A decade and more after the Revolution, Abu Taleb wrote of the new threat that Napoleon posed to Europe.

Abu Taleb sailed to Malta, passing by the island of Corsica where Napoleon had been born. Malta was then administered by monks and their leader was called the Grand Master. When Abu Taleb reached Turkey, he found Constantinople a city of beautiful public mosques but none more splendid than the nearly 1,500-year-old Grand Mosque of Sophia. Its dome, he thought, was more magnificent than that of the St. Paul's Cathedral in London and its gallery could seat thousands. He wrote how the Turkish dress was more expensive than any other in the world. Turkish people wore too many clothes; even the men had on as many as five coats at once. The outer ones were made of broadcloth and the inner ones of satin, and this made movement difficult. The Turkish women were allowed a greater degree of freedom than in Persia or India. They could go unveiled or with only a small veil. Abu Taleb presented the Ottoman emperor of Turkey two volumes of a Persian translation of the Arabic dictionary.

Abu Taleb had to cross the desert to reach Baghdad and he travelled through many cities and villages on the way. From Persia he moved to Punjab, taking an overland route, and finally arrived in Calcutta after a long journey that had taken over four years (1799–1803). His account was written down in Persian by scribes called *katibs* in Calcutta. He presented a few to his friends and a copy came to Charles Stewart, an EIC officer who was an Indophile. Stewart translated it into English as *The Travels of Mirza Abu Taleb Khan in Asia, Africa and Europe, during the years 1799, 1800, 1801, 1802 and 1803.*

IV

JOSEPH EMIN

ARMENIAN ADVENTURER

On the physical map of the world, Armenia appears as a mountainous country in western Asia. Its location – Turkey to the west, Iran in the north, and Georgia (for a long time ruled by the Tsars of Russia) to the east and north-east – meant that Armenia was always threatened by its more powerful neighbours. For centuries, Armenia struggled for independence, finding itself always caught between Turkey ruled by the Ottomans and Russia under the Tsars. For a time, even the armies of Persia (Iran) tormented Armenia. This meant that the Armenians were a people always on the move, driven to become refugees and emigrants. Yet this gave them fortitude and the ability to adapt.

Joseph Emin was an Armenian adventurer, who in the late 1750s travelled from Calcutta to London, hoping to pick up the necessary military skills and ability that would enable him to go to Armenia and fight for its independence. Emin's father was a merchant who had come all the way from Armenia to Calcutta, via Iran. From the 1600s, the city had offered a safe haven to Armenians. They thrived as merchants, traders, moneylenders and, on occasion, as power brokers between the leading political figures of the day.

THE BOY FROM ARMENIA

Emin was born in Hamadan in Persia in 1726 but later travelled to Calcutta where his father had already established himself as a businessman. As a boy, Emin had witnessed first-hand the devastation around him in Armenia. He resolved to help win back for Armenia the status of an independent proud nation. Emin was inspired by Israel Ori, a remarkable figure of Armenian history, who had travelled through Europe, seeking support from rulers for Armenia's independence.

Emin's circumstances were poorer and more precarious than Ori's, but his dreams made him travel from Calcutta to various European countries and Russia. As he later recounted in his memoirs, Emin sought help first from Armenian chiefs and then from the king of Georgia, but it was of no use. He was just a one-man army.

LEAVING FOR ENGLAND

It was in Calcutta, where the British military had an impressive presence, that Emin soon realized that for the Armenians to regain their independence, they needed to be educated and skilled in the art of warfare. In 1751, against the wishes of his father, who threatened to disown him if he followed through with his intentions, an idealistic Emin left for London, hoping to win high officials in the government over to the cause of Armenia's independence.

He left as one of the most junior sailors in the crew, on a ship called *The Walpole*, anchored at Balasore in present-day Odisha. Soon after, he found himself deeply despised by the crew, for he was seen as an 'outsider'. Sailors then mostly spoke Portuguese and Emin had only a basic knowledge of the language. One day a seaman, while handing down bags of rice in the main hatchway, hurled some abusive language at Emin. The latter, unwilling to swallow this humiliation, brought down the man who was three times his size. The other seamen, of whom some were English, were impressed and likened the contest to the biblical one between the boy David and the far stronger Goliath.

Before he left for Europe, Emin wrote to Herakles, or Erekle II, who was then the king of Georgia, and whom Emin saw as a saviour of the Armenians. After the Persian king Nadir Shah's death in 1747, Herakles had liberated his country from Persian rule and re-established the Georgian kingdom. Emin saw Herakles as the great hope who would help liberate Armenia as well.

Emin offered his services to Herakles. In a letter, he wrote to the king about his intentions to travel to England. Emin indulged in a little flattery, praising Herakles's recent victory over the Persian army, and expressed his own desire to join his service. He would help Herakles 'strengthen and polish' his kingdom, and suggested that if Herakles could gather together the thousands of Armenians scattered worldwide, his kingdom could become the most powerful of all.

Emin's first four years in London, however, were filled with misery and hard labour.

LONELY DAYS IN ENGLAND

In the beginning, he tried very hard to seek employment. He was advised to register himself at an office where people made requests for employable people, as servants. Every day for a week he was sent to different gentlemen who wanted to 'interview' him and Emin dutifully set off, quelling his hunger and the cold as best as he could. But he found work only as a bricklayer and then a stevedore, loading and unloading ships at the dock. This was back-breaking, but it allowed him to fend for himself.

Emin then went to work for a lawyer. The lawyer, Mr Webster, knowing that Emin had a 'tolerable hand', employed him as a writer to copy down in detail cases for future reference.

Emin copied cases of lawsuits for about six weeks. He was fond of adding quotes by great figures: Peter the Great of Russia, Charles the Twelfth of Sweden, and other powerful rulers. Mr Webster was obliged to scratch these out and, one day, he paid Emin his wages and politely told him to leave. It was after this that Emin went to work at a grocery.

THE TURNING POINT

In 1755, Emin had the good fortune of meeting the famous statesman and writer Edmund Burke. It was an accidental meeting in a park and Burke gave Emin valuable advice on the books he must read. Having realized Emin's circumstances, Burke also promised to make the necessary introductions for him.

In a second stroke of good luck, Emin's knowledge of horses stood him in good stead when he had a chance encounter with the Duke of Northumberland. The Duke helped him secure admission to the prestigious Royal Military Academy at Woolwich. He remained there for 13 months after which he enlisted as a volunteer to fight for the British and Prussian armies during the Seven Years War against France (1756–1763).

FIRST VISIT TO ARMENIA

In 1759, as the Seven Years War between England and France still raged, Emin decided to head for Armenia. His plan was to travel towards Turkey and then make his way eastward to Armenia. Emin left London, intending to travel all the way to Echmiadzin (now Vagharshapat, one of Armenia's largest cities). But when he reached Leghorn, a port city in Italy, the man who had promised to help him, one Mr Kinlock, shipped himself off to Aleppo in Syria, leaving Emin stranded.

Emin remained in Leghorn for six weeks till the English governor of Leghorn come to his aid. He offered to give Emin an 'Imperial Passport', seeing which the Turks would let him travel unquestioned. It mentioned Emin's occupation as a botanist who collected rare plant specimens to study.

A BOTANIST IN ALEPPO

A grateful Emin reached Aleppo in three days. In a week's time, he bought three horses, hired three Armenian servants, and set out with a large caravan, just as winter began. His destination was directly to the north – the mountains of Armenia. The rain, however, did not let up, and in seven or eight days, turned into snow. Emin knew he had the instruments of guidance – a compass and a map, which he called 'the fruits of European wisdom' – securely in his pocket and he did not deviate from his journey one bit.

In every village he passed, he was shown great respect by the Turks. He showed not the slightest fear. The Turks thought he was a great Armenian, who had risen to become a favourite of the Ottoman sultan, with a '*firman*' (royal command) in his possession.

Emin's initial strategy for liberating Armenia was to motivate the people of the small principalities of Armenia to take up arms. However, his early efforts were a disappointment. A frustrated Emin decided to return to London. But in about eight months' time again, he left London for a second attempt. In October 1761, he decided to head for Russia.

A JOURNEY TO RUSSIA

Some months before, in early 1761, the Russian ambassador in England, Prince Golitsyn, had put Emin in touch with the Russian Imperial Chancellor or prime minister, Count Vorontsov in St. Petersburg (then Russia's capital). Emin secured a letter of recommendation from Vorontsov, and in 1763, Emin entered Tiflis (now Tbilisi, the capital of Georgia), hoping the letter would convince Herakles of his intentions.

Emin set out in a sledge, for it was already winter. At Astrakhan, in western Russia, he received news of heavy snowfall blocking the passes in the Caucasus Mountains in Central Asia. They would open only in June.

Yet, unwilling to delay further, Emin sent a messenger with a letter to Herakles. It would be five months before Emin received Herakles's reply, saying that the Armenians would only serve under him. This was a clear message to Emin that Herakles would tolerate no rival to his own leadership. Emin stayed put for about nine months at Astrakhan.

Finally, having rallied about 30 Armenian men, who joined him with their arms and horses, Emin left Astrakhan once again for Kizlar, a town on Russia's border with Georgia. More Armenians joined the party now, but more out of curiosity and as spectators. Five days after leaving Kizlar, Emin and his men were obliged to halt for a fortnight again on account of the snow. He had to settle with mountain tribes who demanded money to allow them to go across.

THE SUSPICIOUS KING

In Tiflis, Emin finally met Herakles for the first time. Emin stressed the historical links between the Armenian and Georgian people. Emin promised him that a small, disciplined army could easily cross over into Armenia, where a general revolt against Persian and Ottoman rule would ensure that things fell into place. King Herakles showed some enthusiasm for Emin's plans. Emin promised to devote himself to Herakles's service. The king appeared to be vastly pleased with all this.

However, Herakles's suspicion of Emin remained. Well, soon enough, Emin was imprisoned by Herakles's men, who rifled through his belongings. His books, clothes and papers were all returned, but Herakles kept the letters Emin had received from important people in England and Russia.

Emin lost heart. He went on southward and reached Basra in Mesopotamia (now Iraq; then under Ottoman rule). He waited here for about nine months before he set sail homeward for Bengal, in a small ship called *Success*. It took him three months and, one day, just before sunrise, he arrived at his father's door.

ANOTHER, LAST ATTEMPT

After his failed attempt to persuade Herakles, Emin tried to secure financial assistance from Armenian merchants in India for his cause. But he faced opposition once again, from the clergy who had influence among the Armenian merchants and no confidence in Emin's ambitions. Deeply disillusioned, he joined the British Army at the time when Warren Hastings was Governor General of the East India Company at Calcutta. Emin remained in India for the rest of the life, though he never gave up the idea of Armenian independence.

Emin set about writing his memoirs in which he described his many adventures. The book called *Life and Adventures of Joseph Emin, 1726–1809,* was first published in London in 1792. Later, a second edition was prepared and published in Calcutta in 1918 by one of Emin's great-granddaughters who also added all the letters written by Emin in English. When he died, in August 1809, he was buried in the churchyard of Nazareth's Armenian Church in Calcutta.

V

ARDASEER CURSETJEE

ENTERPRISING ENGINEER

He came from a family of shipbuilders who were widely known for their skills in Bombay and he was expected to follow in their footsteps, but Ardaseer (also spelled Ardeshir) Cursetjee was also keen on other subjects, such as the physical sciences and mechanics. He was an extraordinary genius and this was recognized by British, under whom he came to work.

Curstejee's unique gift as an innovator, especially in harnessing steam power, was acknowledged by his superiors. He travelled to London to find out more about the wondrous uses of steam. Ardaseer wrote about his long and cumbersome journey by sea and land to England, with several hilarious moments.

A FAMOUS SHIPBUILDING FAMILY

It was one of Ardaseer's ancestors, Lowjee Nusserwanjee (1700–1774), who first came to prominence as a shipwright or master shipbuilder in Surat, Gujarat. Surat was then famous as a port and, naturally, as a hub for shipbuilders. The master attendant at Surat – an officer who helped in fitting out and equipping ships with the necessary machinery needed for their operation – was impressed with Lowjee's efforts when he worked on building a ship called the *Queen* for the East India Company (EIC). He was invited to Bombay (now Mumbai) in 1735 as the EIC wanted to develop a shipbuilding yard in Bombay.

His sons became shipbuilders too, as did the generations that followed. Between 1812 and 1817, sixteen men-of-war or warships were designed and built in Bombay, as well as 40 other large ships, all under the supervision of Lowjee and his family. *The Minden*, launched in 1810, was the first man-of-war to be built out of England and in Bombay for the British Royal Navy. Ships could be built more cheaply in Bombay and teak, the local timber, lasted longer than English oak. For 150 years, the Wadias, as this shipbuilding family now came to be called, distinguished themselves. The word 'wadia' (also spelled 'vadia') in Arabic and even Gujarati, meant 'carpenter' or 'shipbuilder'.

A PRODIGY IN THE MAKING

In 1822, when he was fourteen, Ardaseer Cursetjee came to work in Bombay, following the family tradition. Here, he designed and supervised the construction of several shipping vessels.

However, his more enduring interest lay in steam machinery. In 1820, even before he joined the shipyard, he had built an engine with a horsepower of 1.

In England, new exciting discoveries with steam were being made right then. Steam was first harnessed by the inventor James Watt to pull loads way faster and better than the horses then in use for this. Ardaseer had a steam engine installed at his home to help pump water up from a well. It was a time when his interest matched the East India Company's as well. In the 1830s, different groups were lobbying for the establishment of a shorter route to Europe and Great Britain, through a canal via the Suez peninsula in Egypt, which would link the Red Sea with the Mediterranean. This route would cut down the earlier long sea journey by over a 1,000 miles (around 1,600 km) and be advantageous for trade.

The EIC officials, seeing Ardaseer's potential, agreed to sponsor his training in steam engineering first at the Bombay Mint in 1831. The Mint, where currency coins were made, was an ideal place for Ardaseer to devote himself to the study of steam machinery. His skills were evident from the fact that soon after acquiring a 10 HP steam engine from England, he had it installed in a boat he designed and built himself. He called it *The Indus* and it was launched in 1833. This was one of the first private steamers built at Bombay.

The Indus was used for demonstrating the advantages of steam technology. Steam would not only benefit shipping but could also be used for irrigation, a significant breakthrough in an agricultural country. From Assistant Builder, he became in-charge at Mazagaon, and soon enough in 1837, the British Indian Navy announced its decision to create an 'all-steam fleet'.

A FASCINATION WITH STEAM

Cursetjee's genius for invention and his fascination with technology stretched to other areas as well. In 1834, he demonstrated how gas could be used as a fuel for domestic lighting in Bombay. He lit up, at his own expense, his own house and garden, and generously invited the public to see this. Hundreds came from miles away to witness this unique event in the city, and even the Governor of Bombay, the Earl of Clare, came with his entourage. After gas lights had been introduced in London's Pall Mall, by 1807 these had already displaced oil lamps in most areas of London. Ardaseer was awarded an 'honorary dress' by the Governor as a gesture of his admiration.

Though Ardaseer's first request to visit Britain did not receive a response, he made a rather mysterious visit to China first; its purpose was revealed much later when he travelled to England in 1839. He sailed on the steamship *Berenice*, leaving behind his family of a wife and three children.

Ardaseer Cursetjee's *Diary of an Overland Journey from Bombay to England and of a Year's Residence in Great Britain*, was published in 1840 in London. It provides a detailed and clear account of his year and a half away from Bombay. A copy of the book was rediscovered around a decade ago by Ardaseer's great-great-grandson in England, Blair Southerden.

Ardaseer was a devout Parsi and so he travelled with servants who prepared his meals on board. During his stay in England he had to decline many invitations for the food would then have been prepared by someone not of his own faith.

A LONG OVERLAND JOURNEY

Ardaseer's overland journey to England began by sea from Bombay. The passengers were to disembark at the port of Suez before proceeding overland on horse or mule to Cairo and Alexandria from where another vessel was to take them via the Mediterranean on to England. This shortened the sea journey by more than a month.

Ardaseer set sail on 13 September 1839. That first evening at sea he wrote of sighting the lighthouse on Colaba Island, which could be seen a long way away from the coast. It made him instantly homesick. Apart from him, there were 20 other passengers. Initially, the strong windy conditions made him quite seasick. The waves rose very high, and the vessel heaved and moved.

Ten days later, they found themselves close to the island of Socotra (Aden) in the northern Indian Ocean. The sky was clear and it was such a beautiful evening that the ladies danced on board. The next day, there were gale-force winds and it took the ship two weeks before it could sight land around Aden. At 2 am, the ship fired a gun and sent up rockets that made blue lights appear in the sky. This was a signal of arrival and that the ship had peaceful intentions. From Aden, it took another week as they sailed up the Red Sea to anchor at the harbour of Suez.

ACROSS THE ARABIAN DESERT

From Suez, however, the passage turned to be a bit tedious, as Ardaseer described it. Though the weather was delightful, for it was winter in the desert, the immediate task to procure a carriage drawn by horses or mules to cross the desert to Cairo and Alexandria proved onerous.

Soon after, on a carriage drawn by four horses, they set off from Suez in the afternoon. The Italian driver had some difficulty in managing his horses through the town's roads. But once in the desert, they made up the distance speedily. The horses had to stop every two hours. By six in the evening, Ardaseer and his fellow travellers had reached the second stage of the journey.

Later in the evening they set off again, this time with four camels pulling the carriage. They passed two rest houses on the way, but they were terrible, infested by fleas, and the odour of horses pervaded everything.

It got progressively darker and Ardaseer's caravan lost its way. They had to stop the carriage right where they were, and some of the men set off with lanterns to find the track they had veered off. Much later, they reached the next station; again the accommodation was uncomfortable and Ardaseer chose to drive on. However, the camels needed to rest for at least three hours. Finally, the Italian pieced together a bed for Ardaseer and his fellow travellers, using the cushion of the carriage and a blanket. But Ardaseer still found plenty to complain about, including the fleas and the mosquitoes.

They resumed their journey very early the next morning. It was almost midnight the next day when they reached Cairo, only to find the entry gates to the city shut. When all their pleas fell on deaf ears, one of them offered a bribe to the Egyptian soldiers and they found themselves in the narrow and lofty streets of the famed city. Ardaseer and his companions spent three days in Cairo before leaving for Alexandria. At Alexandria, they would resume their journey to the island of Malta in the Mediterranean.

STORMS AND SICKNESS IN THE MEDITERRANEAN

It was 21 October and Ardaseer had already been away from Bombay for nearly 40 days. Two days later, early in the morning, they saw the lights of Malta. They had to wait at Fort Manuel on the island for nearly 20 days in quarantine as cholera raged on the island. Though it was almost as if they were imprisoned, the Fort commanded fine views and their rooms were large and comfortable.

On 14 November, they set off again. They passed the coast of Algiers to north Africa in four days and soon Spain was in sight as well. Four days later, they saw the famous Rock of Gibraltar, and it was around midnight that they anchored by the pier.

They changed ships again and this time on 21 November they were in the *Braganza*, headed for England. Cadiz in south-west Spain was a splendid old historic town and they stopped here before moving on to Lisbon, in the choppy seas.

Their ship entered the river Tagus, by which they could enter Lisbon. The weather continued to be rough, even when the ship moved on to the Bay of Biscay, in the west of France. It was the end of November and the sea waves were as high as mountains. But the next day, Ardaseer finally glimpsed the English coast and the lighthouse at Lizard Point in Cornwall.

WINING LAURELS IN ENGLAND

Ardaseer's work in London won him great recognition. He was admitted to several prestigious British institutions and was even elected a Fellow of the Royal Society, the first Indian ever to be thus honoured. He was also made a member of the Society of Arts and Science. In his diary, he wrote about attending several important occasions. He witnessed how the main city was illuminated when Queen Victoria married Prince Albert in February 1840. He was also formally 'presented' to her in court in July that year.

Ardaseer also appeared before a special committee of the House of Commons, the lower house of the British

Parliament. The committee had been set up on the matter of the opium trade with China, and British merchants wanted the government to intervene in what they called was the 'restriction on free trade' by the Chinese government. Many merchants from Bombay were also prominent in this trade. Indeed, six months before Ardaseer's departure for England in 1839, local officials at Canton had seized over 20,000 bales of opium from British and Indian merchants. Merchants argued that such measures were against the principles of 'free trade'. Ardaseer was questioned by the Committee for he knew well about the Bombay merchants and their trading activities. The Committee's findings influenced the decisive action the British government took in support of its own merchants.

Ardaseer spent a lot of time drawing up plans for marine steam engines, working with the firm of Seawards in Milwall, England. Seawards was a reputed marine engineering company established in 1824. Ardaseer had been keen to work in a Thames shipbuilding yard, a place where steamboats and marine engines were built, for this would aid similar innovations in India.

The different dockyards in London and along the Thames were all linked by the railways and canals, and engineers had plentiful opportunities. Ardaseer also made time to visit his cousins Jehangeer Nowrojee and Hirjeebhoy Merwanjee who had preceded him to England and were training as naval architects at the Chatham Naval Dockyard.

He was not, however, full of praise for all things in England. He complained strangely about London's 'dirty roads' (which other writers had called clean), and he thought these were quite unfavourable in contrast to Bombay. He felt London's cab drivers (the small carriage drivers) were insolent and the shopkeepers and tradesmen had the habit of deriding each other, especially when they were in the same business, confusing the unwary customer, especially the foreigner.

A SECOND JOURNEY

It was during his stay in England that an advertisement in *The Times* newspaper caught his eye, inviting applications for the position of Chief Engineer and Inspector of Machinery at the steam factory and foundry in Bombay. Ardaseer swiftly applied and a month later he was unanimously chosen by the EIC for the job. He became the first Indian to be employed by the EIC, who would supervise Europeans.

Ardaseer Cursetjee worked at this post in Bombay for 16 years. In February 1851 he helped launch the steamship *Lowjee Family*, built by his son Rustomjee Ardeshir at Mazagaon Dock, the same place where Ardaseer had started work.

VISITING THE UNITED STATES

That same year (though some accounts place this in 1849), he made a second visit to England, but this time he went to the United States first. He did not write about his travels here, but Caroline Howard King, the daughter of his hosts in Salem, Massachusetts, wrote of Ardaseer's visit in her memoir, *When I Lived in Salem*, published in 1837. In 2003, poet Mustansir Dalvi wrote of Caroline's description of the meeting in this poem:

A REAL LIVE PARSEE

'We were startled one evening
by a friend's bringing
a real live Parsee,
with a tall calico headdress,
and an Oriental long coat,
to take tea with us.

It was rather a revelation to me
that a fire worshipper could take tea
like ordinary mortals.

Ardeshir Cursetji Wadia
(O how we giggled trying to say that later)
was a harmless lion,
who roared very gently,
and sipped his tea
and ate his bread and butter
quite like Salem good folk.
We talked of several things
of teak, and hulls and men o' war,
of audiences with the Queen,

of Duncan Dock in Bombay,
and all the places he'd been.

I remember we all spoke
very distinctly, as if we were talking to a child,
and that he answered us
in a very low cultivated refined voice,
using much better English than we'.

– © Mustansir Dalvi; First published in *Brouhahas of Cocks*, by Poetrywala, 2013

On his return to Bombay in February 1853, Ardaseer brought back with him from the US some wood-cutting machinery and items related to photography. He is credited with introducing photography and electroplating to Bombay. This technique makes metal resistant to rust formation and was another innovation he introduced to India's fledging manufacturing industry. It was in this year that the first photographic society was formed in India, and Ardaseer Cursetjee was one of the founding members.

Soon enough, he did travel back to England, this time for good. He made his home in Richmond, a suburb of London. In May 1969 the Indian Post and Telegraph department issued a stamp in his honour, on which his portrait is shown with the sailing ships he so loved working with.

VI
ISHUREE DASS
MISSIONARY MAN

Ishuree Dass was a scholar and a missionary who travelled to England and later to the United States. He had been raised by missionaries for he had lost his parents when he was very young. Dass was from Futtehguhr (Fatehgarh) in the United Provinces (now Uttar Pradesh). He was raised under the care of the missionary H.R. Wilson, and it was with Wilson that he travelled to England and the US in 1846. Besides being familiar with many languages such as English, Persian and Urdu, Dass was also a teacher and he travelled to be trained in theology and other subjects of religious instruction. He published his book called *A Brief Account of a Voyage to England and America* on his return in 1851. It was the first account in English written by an Indian traveller to the United States.

THE OLD SAILING SHIPS

Dass sailed from Calcutta in the *Tudor*, a large English vessel, on 16 February 1846. The *Tudor* was a three-masted full sailing ship, with square sails. It was not one of the new steam vessels that had recently begun to appear in the seas, nor was it a clipper, one of the sailing ships that set a fast pace in the sea.

The eight cabins on the upper deck were the most comfortable and expensive. The 40 on the second deck were less convenient and less expensive too. To Dass, the sailors on board looked like wild men at first, and even appeared ferocious when compared to the poor boatmen of his homeland. But in the days he spent on board the ship, he found them to be hardworking and courageous. Besides the passengers, there were some 'insane' soldiers on board, who were being sent to England to recover. The journey to England took around two months.

AROUND LONDON

Dass fell into the habit of walking around in London and amusing himself with the novel sights he saw everywhere. Walking, it seemed to him, was a common habit, and Londoners always carried their umbrellas for the weather could change all of a sudden.

At the same time, using the city's public transport was cheap. There were 'omnibuses' on the main streets, with their names and destinations written clearly on their sides. They followed a set route. At the start of the journey, the omnibuses moved slowly, picking up passengers, and when there was a certain number on board, they picked up pace, and anyone who wanted to get on had to call out to the footman who stood behind the coach. The footman, by pulling a string attached to the vehicle, would draw the driver's attention. There were policemen, on the alert, walking about in the streets.

The cleanliness of London surprised Dass. There were many sweepers' carts going about the roads, gathering garbage from everywhere. The movement of carriages was orderly and people were never in any danger of being run over by them. Occasionally, he also enjoyed an excursion in a steamboat on the Thames.

The Parliament was meeting at London during this time, and Dass once happened to be near the Houses of Parliament just as they assembled for a session. There was already a big crowd eyeing the aristocrats and the parliamentarians with open curiosity as they entered. Suddenly, the Duke of Wellington, the famous soldier who had defeated Napoleon at the battle of Waterloo in 1815, was sighted and the crowds raised a loud cheer in his honour.

EYE-OPENING WONDERS

At the British Museum, Dass was impressed by the dark, venerable sculptures from Egypt and the statues of some of the old Roman orators.

The Egyptian mummies were one of the wonders of their age, and were housed in a special chamber of the museum. There were mounted birds too, of every colour, size and description, and from every region and climate. There were also snakes and serpents of all sizes, even the most monstrous. He came across a stuffed rhinoceros too, its body riddled by bullet marks. And among the other great curiosities was the skeleton of a large and mighty beast, bigger than even an elephant. Dass did not mention the mammoth by name but wrote that such skeletons were found embedded in ice in some extremely cold regions in the north. Appreciating all the marvels in the British Museum, Dass wrote, required one to set aside several months.

The Thames Tunnel was the greatest fascination of modern times. This was a passageway built under the bed of the river Thames. It was dug deep, and there were many steps that led to the bottom. The roof of the tunnel was a double arch supported by columns in the middle. The tunnel was always damp considering the volume of water that rolled over it constantly. It was also quite dark inside, so it was lit up at all times. There were several shops all along the tunnel, which sold fruit, toys and other knick-knacks. It amused him, he wrote, to be walking in this passage, while ships were sailing over one's head.

It was in London for the first time that he saw gas being used to produce light. It was conveyed to houses via underground iron pipes. The houses were supplied water in the same manner.

TRAVELLING BY TRAIN IN AMERICA

Towards the end of August 1846, Dass sailed for America. A month later at sea, they encountered the most dreadful storm, just when the ship was off the coast of Newfoundland in Canada. When a storm broke out in the 'awful deep', the ship was continually lashed by angry waves as high as mountains. It shook like a leaf; the masts strained and almost bent at the fearful force of the wind. By the next morning though, to everyone's relief, the storm had passed.

On 4 October, almost a month later, the ship dropped anchor in the harbour of New York. This was a large city, though, as Dass noted, nothing in comparison to London in that period, and in terms of population, even to Calcutta. It was a city of busy traffic and its buildings and streets aroused great admiration in him for those who responsible for the city's creation.

Dass then set out for Philadelphia, a distance of about 100 miles (around 160 km) from New York. With Reverend Wilson, he was to travel by railroad, an innovation in transport in those days. The station was very crowded, for this train ran between two of the biggest and most populous American cities, New York and Philadelphia. The carriages were built like a palanquin carriage. The seats inside, covered with velvet, were placed in short double rows, and each had room for two persons. These seats had a narrow aisle in the middle as well. The train reached Philadelphia six hours later. Today, this same journey takes only an hour or so.

Dass's attention was drawn to the verdant landscape through which they passed. America appeared to be a huge country, and large parts were still uninhabited. Here and there he did see a few houses, or even a barn and a cottage, but no town or even a village.

A COLLEGE IN AMERICA

In Pennsylvania, the state in which Philadelphia is located, Dass spent most of his time at Easton, at Lafayette College. He described Easton as 'one of the best small places' he had ever seen. The houses were neat, large and comfortable, and there were many shops where every article of comfort could be bought. In the centre of the town was the Court House that added to its beauty.

The Colchester Academy, where Dass was a student though he was a few years older than his peers here, was intended to prepare students for college. It offered instruction in Greek, Latin, English Literature and Mathematics to the scholars.

There was a large class of Latin Grammar, another devoted to the Latin Reader, a third to Caesar's commentaries, while some other students studied Virgil, a Latin poet and scholar. Another class also studied Algebra, and a few students Geometry, or English. Recreation involved walking in the beautiful countryside around Easton. Their greatest source of amusement and exercise was ball-playing and in winter they threw snowballs at one another.

After appearing for the examination, Dass left Easton for Winchester, further south in the state of Virginia. This was in the late 1840s and Virginia, like other southern States, was still a 'slave state'. He wrote that it was common to see two or three or even more slaves owned by most families. Some farmers had as many as four or five hundred slaves working on their farms.

WHAT AMERICANS KNEW ABOUT HINDUSTAN

It took almost an entire day's journey to reach Winchester. The people of Winchester had heard of the arrival of a 'foreigner from a distant country' and they were curious. Those that had some acquaintance with Dass's host family came to meet him and were surprised that he could speak English, or that he did not show any signs of the 'savagery' they expected. Dass wrote that most Americans had a very poor and ridiculous idea of India. He was amazed at the questions he was asked at times. It was like he was a 'traveller from the Moon' for they seemed to know nothing about India or, indeed, much about the rest of the world.

He went on to explain how this ignorance came about from the geography they were taught. In a textbook he came across, nearly three-fourths of the pages were about their own country. The lessons on America took up 133 pages, while only 41 pages were devoted to Europe, 26 to Asia and 22 to Africa.

Hindustan was described as a beautiful country in Asia, which was famous for its ancient civilization, and also its valuable products. It was also known for its many rivers and fertile soils that allowed two crops to be cultivated in a year, the most important being rice, cotton, wheat, sugar, indigo, opium, tobacco, millet and fruits.

AMERICAN LIFESTYLES

The houses in America (as well as in England) were almost always built identically and uniformly in well-arranged rows, not in a haphazard manner as in India. A brass plate on every door had the house number or the name of resident engraved on it.

In the northern US states slavery had already been abolished and servants were scarce. In the south, he found that the slaves were generally treated with kindness. But when Dass asked an old woman slave if she found her position comfortable or preferred freedom, she chose the latter.

He wrote about the boarding system that was popular in America. Married people who owned a home found it practical to take in a boarder in their house. This brought in extra income. Often married couples too would rent two or three rooms in a house and pay a sum to the owner's family for their meals. In this way, they did not have to bother with housekeeping.

ELECTIONS AND EDUCATION

Dass saw how the Americans conducted elections. In most countries, including India, which was then ruled by the British, there were never any elections. The first elections would be held in India more than a century later, after independence, in 1952. In America, Dass saw that a great many people had assembled in the post office. At election time, orators delivered speeches in favour of candidates they preferred. Sometimes there were very vocal disagreements. The elections were conducted by ballot: people wrote their choice on a piece of paper, and it was placed in a box and later counted.

He found the Americans 'enterprising, energetic and industrious' and predicted that if they continued in the same spirit that had impelled them thus far, America would in course of time 'be a most glorious country'.

On 11 August 1847, he left for Calcutta on board a British ship called the *Coromandel*. Around the end of January, he happily found himself back in the City of Palaces, as Calcutta was then called.

Later, Dass worked as headmaster in a school in Farrukhabad and another school in Rakhal. He wrote works in Urdu on grammar, geography and history. Besides his travelogue, he also wrote a book on essential Hindustani verbs and their English equivalents, and yet another on the local manners and customs of Hindustan for those who might have come to India recently from England.

VII

JEHANGEER NOWROJEE AND HIRJEEBHOY MERWANJEE

SHIPBUILDING COUSINS

The first half of the 19th century – the period 1800–1850 – could be seen as the golden age of shipbuilding. In China, under the great admiral Zheng He, and Europe – especially the kingdoms of Spain and Portugal first – the sailing ships of the 14th and 15th centuries, which had led to the great voyages of exploration, now gave way to faster and sleeker ships. It was Britain that led the way. Following the use of steam and the speeding up of the Industrial Revolution, steamships began to be built in large numbers. It was an exciting time for shipbuilders and those keen on the science of navigation.

Jehangeer Nowrojee and Hirjeebhoy Merwanjee belonged to one of Bombay's best-known shipbuilding families. They were cousins, who belonged to the Parsi community, and were also related to Ardaseer Cursetjee, an inventor and shipbuilder himself. Being shipbuilders, they travelled to England to learn more about shipbuilding at the Chatham Dockyard.

This dockyard, located on the River Medway, was set up when England was at war nearly 400 years ago with other countries in Europe. Since that time the dockyard at Chatham had provided more than 500 ships for the British Navy, and was at the forefront of shipbuilding technology. The cousins left for London on 29 March 1838. In their travelogue, they provide an eyewitness account of the tremendous progress Britain had made in several fields.

THE MAGIC OF STEAM

At the time they travelled, steam was being used more and more often for sailing; huge steam vessels now sailed longer distances across oceans.

The cousins left on board the *Buckinghamshire*, with a friend who was more like a guide or adviser to them, and two servants, all from the Parsi community. The route they took was the long one down the west coast of India, past the

Indian Ocean, passing the Cape of Good Hope at the very tip of Africa and then moving northward to the Atlantic.

Their fellow passengers suffered from seasickness in the initial days of the journey. But the cousins felt not the slightest symptoms, and for this they thanked the simple lifestyle they had adopted while at sea. They ate simple food and had hardly any wine, and this helped.

THE LONELY ISLAND

On the morning of 6 July 1838, after over three months at sea, they sighted the island of St. Helena, which they had heard about from other travellers on this route. It appeared as a huge rock standing in the middle of the wide ocean. The island's main town, Jamestown, had a population of around four thousand. This barren and lonely place was where Napoleon Bonaparte was exiled in 1816.

On the afternoon of 10 July they passed Ascension Island. A few more weeks later, their ship arrived at Dover on the south-east coast of England. The cliffs at Dover were high and chalky, and Dover Castle stood at its highest point. The town of Dover was important to the military for it guarded the entrance to the rivers Thames and Medway. The town's fortifications had been improved many times, especially when the French Revolution broke out in 1789.

The cousins were amazed at the numbers of ships sailing down the Thames. These ships were of all kinds – colliers, timber ships, merchantmen, steamers, and crafts from all parts of the world. What was astounding to them was also the fact that these ships plied on the Thames, which was not really a big river but 'a stream' compared to the Ganges and the Indus. It was a great wonder to them that England, which appeared as relatively tiny on the world map could draw in so many nations of the world, as represented by their ships, towards her.

AMAZEMENT, BOTHWAYS

On 27 August 1838, their ship arrived at the Gravesend docks, and the cousins boarded a smaller steam vessel in order to sail ahead to London. This was the first time they had ever travelled on a steam vessel and the spacious accommodation impressed them. The steamer travelled at a rate of 11 miles an hour, and the music that played on board was delightful. It was nearly dusk when they arrived in London. Instantly a crowd flocked round them, intrigued by their clothes. The two cousins, their friend, and their helps gathered around them quite a mob, making it difficult for them to move towards their carriage.

A few days later, the cousins went to an exhibition called the Diorama. This presented a most extraordinary optical illusion. On entering, they saw the inside of a spacious building, almost like the interior of a huge church. While they looked on, this became enveloped in flames and was destroyed in no time. The fire raged till all the decorations and fittings had burned down and the place was a mass of charred ruins. It then became clear that it was all an illusion managed with a magic lantern with lenses of high power.

The zoo in London had almost every animal from all around the world. The elephant was so docile and obedient to his keeper that he handed over a small amount of money to a person who sold cakes and also received some coins in exchange. The bears too were amusing. They were in a deep pit in the centre of which there was a wooden pole of wood. The bears kept crawling up this to receive cake from the spectators. Having grasped it, they slid back down the pole just like sailors down a rope. The monkeys too appeared delighted to be taken notice of.

While walking around the zoo, the cousins attracted a lot of attention, because of the very peculiarity of their dress – the traditional Parsi turban and long kurta. They were as much objects of curiosity as the winged and four-footed inmates of the place. Many in the crowd made guesses about where they could have come from: someone called them Chinese, another said they were Turks, and still others insisted they were Spanish.

COUNTING CARRIAGES

At any given time in London city one could see a large number of horse carriages, all of different descriptions. The largest of these were the omnibuses. Nearly 700 of these ran in every direction all day. As the two cousins were engineers, they tended to make estimations of everything. Some of these omnibuses, they calculated, performed their journeys four times a day, and thus passed a given spot eight times each day. These were built to carry 12 or 14 persons inside, who sat in facing rows. The omnibuses were fitted up very nicely inside, their seats lined with velvet either red or green in colour.

Although the omnibus was drawn by two horses, every proprietor who owned two omnibuses was obliged to keep at least seven horses, so that the animals could get adequate rest. There were also a huge number of smaller carriages drawn by two horses, called the hackney coaches, and still smaller ones pulled by a single horse, called cabs. The law had fixed what the drivers could charge and they were fined heavily if they overcharged.

The cousins visited an exhibition of waxwork figures at a place in Baker Street. This was the famous Madame Tussaud's, still a very popular draw in London. They described the great many figures displayed, as large as life, dressed exactly in the costume the persons they were modelled on wore daily. These were so very lifelike that when the room was crowded with visitors it became very difficult to distinguish the living from the wax representations.

TIME TRAVEL IN TRAINS

Since Jehangeer and Hirjeebhoy had come to England to pick up certain skills, first in English and Maths, they soon found the right teacher for this. Their teacher, who was also a clergyman, lived in Egham in Buckinghamshire, a county some distance from London. They went to see him and to look at a house they wanted to rent for their stay in England. To reach Egham, they had to travel by train along the west coast of England, passing places like Bath, Bristol, Gloucester and Cheltenham. What amazed them was the speed at which the train travelled. Within an hour, while they were seated quietly in a beautiful carriage, the train was already 25 miles (around 40 km) away from London.

The rail carriages were of two kinds: those of the first-class were fitted up beautifully with cushions and glass windows. The seats accommodated three persons on each side. Some coaches had a lamp inside for night travelling. The second-class carriages were fitted only with benches.

MIND-BOGGLING SIGHTS

At an exhibition held in a polytechnic in London, they reported seeing some of the most impressive technological marvels of the day. These included machines for cultivating the earth: agricultural instruments such as ploughs, harrows, rakes, threshing machines and drills to sow seeds. They saw a pneumatic telegraph which, when air was passed through a tube, conveyed signals across miles. There was also something called a hydrostatic bed, lying on which patients could move in some comfort, instead of being confined to one position for a considerable length of time on account of illness. They also saw a very ingenious weighing machine, for this was something new then: one sat down in a chair, and a hand, like that of a clock, showed one's weight.

Iron was found abundantly in England. Its production offered employment to many people. Steamboats, steamships and the massive railway network were being built entirely of iron. An entrepreneur had had the idea of having carriages made of iron, for plying on the overland desert route in Egypt. To the cousins, it was clear that England owed a lot of her economic success to the supplies of coal and iron available in that country.

In tune with the times, the knowledge of mechanics was encouraged in almost every small town in England. Many respectable citizens of the town joined workers to hire or build a large room where lectures on subjects connected with the sciences, engineering and mechanics were delivered frequently, either by skilled people in the neighbourhood, or by professional lecturers who came from London.

DAY OUT AT A DAIRY

Laycock's Dairy was located at Islington, near London. It took up 14 acres of land, and within a high wall, more than 400 cows were kept in their separate stalls, for supplying milk. The city of London itself consumed more than eight million gallons of milk annually. The cows were milked twice every day. Their food varied as much as possible: a large species of beetroot constituted their chief food, but they also had turnips, cabbages, carrots and clover. The owner apparently had four farms, all to supply the varied green food required for the cattle. He also had a large number of horses constantly fetching grains, and carting away the manure. All the cows were as sleek as racehorses, and they were brushed down with a comb every day. There was even a hospital for when the cows calved or needed other medical treatment. The milk was taken into a dairy soon after milking. The dairy premises were kept scrupulously clean, and were scoured with hot water twice every day.

The cousins wrote about how the Parliament worked, their visits to Greenwich, and other London sights such as the Tower of London, the Thames Tunnel and St. Paul's Cathedral. At the Tower of London, the crown made for Her Majesty Queen Victoria's coronation had been displayed for the public. There was also a beautiful salt cellar that was used on the royal table on the day of the coronation. It was an exact model of the tower, and an excellent piece of workmanship.

A MEETING WITH THE QUEEN

The cousins travelled to Windsor Castle, one of the queen's royal residences, hoping to see the queen as she took a walk in the castle's beautifully laid out gardens. The castle stood at a somewhat high level and so provided a pretty view for miles round. As they headed to the terrace, they saw that a crowd had already gathered - men, women, and children, dressed in their best clothes, walking around and enjoying the breeze. At about half past four, the band began to play to announce the queen's arrival.

In a few minutes, Queen Victoria appeared on the terrace, a broad tiled expanse that could take in quite a crowd. Everybody arranged themselves on either side of the road to bow or curtsey as she moved down the terrace to pass through the road. She walked past close to where the cousins stood. And then shortly after, one of her attendants came running back to the cousins to ask them who they were and other details such as their country of origin. The cousins, flattered by the attention, gladly supplied this information. But the attendant returned in no time saying that Her Majesty now wanted to know their names. Realizing how difficult their names might sound, they handed over their 'business cards' so the queen might read their names. The cousins noted with some pleasure how the queen had indeed turned back once to look at them and the novelty of their costume.

Accompanied by Ardaseer Cursetjee, their other cousin, they also visited the Woolwich dockyard. This was oldest royal dockyard in England. At Woolwich, there was also an extensive establishment for the manufacture of cannon, fireworks and gun carriages. This was the Royal Arsenal, and one of the furnaces here could melt 17 tonnes of metal at one time.

EDUCATION UNLIMITED

To give an idea of how a middle-class family in England lived, the cousins mentioned their friend, who was a widower with seven daughters. The eldest of them was 16 years old and the youngest was two. Six of these seven daughters were weekly boarders in a school in the neighbourhood. They came home on Saturday at noon and returned to school on

Monday, at nine in the morning. They were taught reading, spelling, grammar, geography and history. They had weekly exams that consisted of their repeating answers to questions on various subjects. A French lady also resided in the house to teach the girls French. A master came to teach them writing and arithmetic, and music was taught alternately by a male and a female teacher. All the six girls who were in school and about 20 others were being taught to dance, to carry themselves well, and to curtsy. This was to teach them how to behave like genteel, well-bred young women.

In general, it was thought that a public education suited boys as it afforded them a spirit of competition. The children of people with small incomes attended schools where for about £4 a year, they received a basic education. For the children of the poor, there were schools maintained by subscriptions from the middle and upper classes of society. In addition, there were Sunday schools for those poor children who were obliged to work for their living on other days. The cousins realized and, indeed, as their journey to England proved, it was education, and the ability to read and write, that helped improve one's life and made it easier to be gainfully and usefully employed.

VIII
TORU DUTT
WRITER'S SIDE

Toru Dutt was born into the well-known and illustrious Dutt family of Calcutta, a family that distinguished itself in literary and educational pursuits. Even as a teenager, Toru was proficient in several languages: Bengali, English, French and also Sanskrit. She left behind an impressive collection of prose and poetry. Her *Le Journal de Mademoiselle d'Arvers* was the first novel in French by an Indian writer while *Bianca, or, The Young Spanish Maiden*, is believed to be the first novel in English by an Indian woman writer. A collection of Toru Dutt's correspondence includes the letters she wrote from England to her cousins in India.

THE DUTTS OF CALCUTTA

The Dutts of Rambagan were an old and well-known family of Calcutta. Toru's father Govin Chunder was greatly influenced by the teachers who taught at the newly formed Hindu College (in 1855, this became the Presidency College). One of his teachers was the poet and scholar Henry Vivian Louis Derozio who stimulated his students by discussing important social, moral, political and religious questions of the day. Govin Chunder knew many languages, a gift inherited by both his daughters, Toru and Aru. He also had a talent for poetry. Some of his early writings and those of his two brothers and a nephew, were published in England in 1870 in a book called *The Dutt Family Album*.

Toru's mother, Kshetramonij Mitter, was well versed in Hindu mythology. She translated *The Blood of Jesus* from English into Bengali, and it was published by the Tract and Book Society of Calcutta. Toru, the youngest of Govin Chunder Dutt's children, was born in Calcutta, on 4 March 1856. Her early years were spent in Calcutta and also in their country house at Baugmaree - at the time, it was just outside the city's precincts. The house here was in the middle of an extensive garden, covering acres of land and shaded by fruit trees.

A TRAGEDY THAT PROMPTED TRAVEL

It was early in the year 1869 that Toru, with her sister Aru, accompanied their parents to Europe. In fact, they were the first Bengali ladies to visit Europe. Three years before there had been a tragedy in the family. In 1865, Toru's brother, Abju, barely fourteen, had died from an unexpected illness, later believed to be tuberculosis (called consumption at the time). The Dutt sisters too were often sick and it was partly to offer their children a healthier environment that the family decided to travel to the West. The family first went by sea to Bombay in a steamer, there being no railway in those days between the two cities. They sailed from Bombay to Aden, and then made the overland journey from Suez to Alexandria. The Suez Canal would open only later that year in November and, on their return, they would sail through it.

Their ship sailed along the Mediterranean and the family landed at Marseilles in the south of France. They spent a few months here. Marseilles was France's second largest city, historically a trade centre and France's chief port. Marseilles saw industrial innovations and a rise in manufacturing in the late 1800s. The Suez Canal that opened in 1869 further aided its growth.

CARNIVAL NIGHT IN NICE

It was at Nice, another city in the south of France that Toru and her sister went to school, at a French *pensionnat* (boarding school). The climate here was cool and temperate, its air was clear and so the family decided to stay for a bit. The school in Nice that they attended would be the only school they ever went to, for they were taught by governesses at home. It was here that they became really proficient in French.

At Nice the Dutts stayed at the Hotel Helvetique. At this time Toru wrote a letter to a young cousin, Arun Chunder Dutt in Calcutta, in which she described her stay at Nice. She showed a keen sense of humour and sharp observational skills. The natural beauty of Nice and its rejuvenating climate drew the English upper classes here. An increasing number of families from the nobility spent their winters in the city. The city's main seaside promenade even came to be called the *Promenade des Anglais* or the 'Walkway of the English'.

Toru told her cousin that when his letter arrived they were dining '*table d'hôte*' (a table at a restaurant that offers meals at fixed prices). Two musicians played on a harp and a violin to give them a *bon appétit*. She described the carnival during which people wore masks, and coloured themselves, and threw bonbons at people. The roads got very muddy in all this excitement.

Their father had hired a carriage to watch the carnival, but it turned out to be a very bad and broken one. As the carriage picked up pace, their mother feared that the roof would soon fall off and they too would be pelted with bonbons. But they reached the city's 'Terrace', a kind of viewing point, without any mishap. While their parents waited in the carriage, Toru, Aru and a family friend called Mr Elliott walked to the terrace to witness the carnival. There were already large crowds gathered and the girls had to stand on chairs to watch the procession. There were soldiers below the terrace to keep order, while other soldiers played the trumpet, the drums and other musical instruments.

Toru and Aru made many friends in Nice, some of whom were from England. They also loved going for long walks on the famous 'Promenade des Anglais'. After several months the Dutts went to Paris. It was a long train journey and they hoped to recuperate by spending some days in this city, even then called 'the capital of the world'.

A LEISURELY JOURNEY

Toru wrote about the charms of Paris to her cousin in Calcutta. It was, she said, the greatest of all cities especially if 'beauty, comfort, climate and cleanliness' were considered. After staying a few days in Paris, they started for England, via Boulogne in the north of France. It was already the spring of 1870. Mr Dutt was determined this time to travel in a more leisurely way.

Boulogne was a quaint old place that, Toru Dutt noted, the English writer William Makepeace Thackeray had written about often. When they arrived there, it appeared a wretched little maritime town with houses apparently built only for sailors. Owing to the fine weather, the family resolved not to delay a moment more but to cross the English Channel at the earliest.

They sailed across the Channel and took the train to London from Folkestone right on the English coast. Compared to the earlier travellers, rail travel was now common here and taken for granted.

LONDON'S HIGH AND MIGHTY

In London they rented a furnished house at Brompton. It was here that Toru began to develop an interest in translating poetry and also wrote her own poems. They became acquainted with the well-known composer George Macfarren, whose wife became the girls' singing teacher. Macfarren had married the famous opera singer and pianist, Clarina Thalia Andrae. She was from Poland, but found success as a concert singer and singing teacher in London.

Toru wrote in her letters about the many people in London she knew from their time in India. Sir Bartle Frere, who had been the governor at Bombay from 1862 to 1867, and his family were known to them. The sisters spent several happy days at the Frere home in Wimbledon. Another friend the Dutts knew by correspondence was Le Chevalier de Chatelain, who was a friend of the famous French writer Victor Hugo. Chatelain was himself a well-known translator of several of Shakespeare's plays and also Chaucer's *Canterbury Tales* into French. There was also Edward Ryan who had been a judge in Calcutta and was a keen supporter of the educational reformer Thomas Macaulay.

The sisters made interesting observations every time they went about in London. As they rode through Orislow Square, and passed Holland House, it reminded them of Lord and Lady Holland. One of the sisters remembered reading about the famous snuffbox that Napoleon of France had presented to Lady Holland. This was now displayed at the British Museum. The poet Lord Byron had ridiculed

Napoleon's gesture in a poem and the Dutt sisters knew of this poem too.

Both Lord and Lady Holland had been great admirers of Napoleon. In 1815, soon after his defeat, Lady Holland had commissioned a bronze bust of Napoleon by the celebrated Italian sculptor Antonia Canova. Even after Napoleon was exiled to the island of St. Helena, Lady Holland sent him supplies of food and many books. Napoleon remembered Lady Holland in his will and after his death in 1821, his cherished gold snuffbox, gifted to him by the Pope, came to her.

Sir Edward Ryan also invited the Dutt sisters to his office where candidates for the Civil Service, those who served as bureaucrats in India, were examined. In the lobby of his house, they saw a bust of Dwarkanath Tagore, the famous poet and Rabindranath Tagore's grandfather. Sir Edward's library 'looked a paradise for a literary man'. Toru described the bookcases that rose to the ceiling, filled with books. On top of them, rolled up inside wooden frames, were maps, which when pulled out would cover and conceal the bookcases and form a sort of geographical tapestry.

On the tables nearby were masks, a crown, daggers, a sword, false beards, periwigs, and all the paraphernalia that was part of theatre performances. Stage productions were frequent in Sir Edward's house and he had been a patron of the theatre when in Calcutta – especially of two of the oldest ones, Chowringhee and Sans Souci.

The Dutt sisters went to the London theatres too. A play they particularly enjoyed was an adaptation of Sir Walter

Scott's *Amy Robsart*. With Sir Edward, they discussed some of the novels of William Makepeace Thackeray and also Anthony Trollope's works that spoke much about ordinary life of the times.

SEASONS IN LONDON

When Toru Dutt wrote to her cousin in Calcutta, she also mentioned the changing seasons. In autumn, the trees were quite bare, except a few. The square outside their window looked very desolate with the shorn trees. She described the robins that appeared every morning when they went for a walk in the square.

As winter came, she wrote of the snow that fell heavily on some days causing her to slip when outside. But it was still very pleasant despite that. The boys out on the streets had fun throwing snowballs at one another and they even pelted passers-by playfully. The Dutt girls had fun playing with snowballs too and they aimed these at their mother's conservatory, or at the chimney.

She wrote of her music lessons as well. Her piano teacher Mr Pauer was teaching her to play *Schmetterlinge* or *Butterflies*. She described it as a very pretty and easy piece. Aru, for her part, was learning a sonata by Mozart.

Toru Dutt had a wonderful memory. She could repeat in the original almost every piece she translated. One had only to repeat a line of the translation and she would be able to recite the original poem in its entirety. She read much and was a very quick reader too. Her father recounted that whenever he had an argument with Toru over the significance of an expression or a sentence in Sanskrit, or French, or German, most times it was Toru who would prove to be right.

She described in detail their daily schedule in London: it was really packed with study, routine activities and practise on the piano.

THE WAR IN FRANCE

Toru followed with deep interest the war of 1871 that engulfed Europe. She hoped very much that England would not embroil itself in the war. Having spent some time in France, she sympathized with the French who had been attacked by the Prussians under Chancellor Bismarck.

When the French armies were defeated in 1871, Toru was devastated. One evening, she overheard her father mention something to her mother. She descended the stairs 'like lightning' only to learn that the French had surrendered to Bismarck's Prussia . The Emperor of France, Napoleon III (Napoleon's nephew, who became King of France in 1852), and his entire army had surrendered at Sedan. Toru ran back up the stairs to break the news to her sister.

They moved to Cambridge and lived there between 1871 and 1873. Toru and her sister began attending the 'Higher Lectures for Women', a programme recently started for women at the university. Toru worked hard on her French during her days in Cambridge, a skill that would serve her well when she wrote her two novels in that language. She was also privately tutored at home in French during the last part of their stay in England. They soon became a familiar sight in Cambridge, as they took their daily walks in the university town.

Toru Dutt also made friends with Mary Martin, the daughter of Reverend John Martin of Sidney Sussex College, founded in 1595, in the University of Cambridge. The friendship that developed between the two girls continued in their correspondence after Toru's return to India. In the September of 1873, the Dutts decided to return to Calcutta in the ship called *Peshawur*. Toru wrote to Mary about their return journey to India. It was a journey that took them through the newly opened Suez Canal.

SAILING THROUGH THE SUEZ

Toru wrote of how their ship was stuck two or three times in the Suez Canal, but only for a few minutes each. The ship sailed at a very slow speed through the canal. The canal was very narrow, and one could see land on either side. The salt lakes looked pretty, and there were hardly any trees or houses to be seen. Only at Ismailia, where the ship anchored for the night, was there some greenery. This town also had houses as the French engineers who worked on the Canal lived here.

Both Toru and Aru suffered from seasickness during the somewhat rough weather at the beginning of their journey. Their pets, though – the guinea pigs and birds that they were bringing back with them – managed well. The Dutts made friends on board, but they were too shy to join in the singing and playing.

The voyage homeward was largely pleasant. Only after they passed Madras did they encounter a few days of bad weather and rain. The steamer was detained for four days at Galle in south-west Ceylon (now Sri Lanka) and that became very tiresome.

BACK HOME IN CALCUTTA

On her return, Toru Dutt resumed the study of Sanskrit together with her father. She came across a book, *La Femme dans Vinde Antique*, written by Clarisse Bader, a French writer of some repute. Toru was so charmed with it that she wrote to the writer, hoping to be allowed to translate it into English for the benefit of Indian readers. The correspondence that ensued developed into a warm friendship between the two women, who though widely separated by geography, were united by a shared love of literary things.

In her letters to Mary Martin, Toru eloquently and painfully mentioned how much they all longed to return to England. But it was not to be. After Aru's death a year later, Toru too succumbed to illness – the tuberculosis that had affected her most of her young life – leaving their parents devastated and grief-stricken.

Her first book of poetry called *A Sheaf Gleaned in French Fields* mainly included her translations of French poetry into English. This was published in Calcutta in 1876. Eight of the poems here were also translated by her sister Aru. In 1877, this volume caught the eye of the well-known poet and critic Edmund Gosse, who had been a mentor to Sarojini Naidu too. Gosse gave the book a favourable review. *A Sheaf*... would see a second Indian edition in 1878 and a third in London in 1880, but Toru did not see any of these successes. Her two novels, the unfinished *Bianca, or, The Young Spanish Maiden* written in English and *Le Journal de Mademoiselle d'Arvers*, written in French and published in 1879, were based outside India with protagonists who were not Indian. These two were also published after her death. A later book that her father got published was called the *Ancient Ballads and Legends of Hindustan*. It includes her translations and adaptations from Sanskrit literature.

In 1882, Edmund Gosse wrote an introductory memoir for it. In this he wrote of Toru Dutt: 'She brought with her from Europe a store of knowledge that would have sufficed to make an English or French girl seem learned, but which in her case was simply miraculous.' He continued: 'If Toru Dutt were alive, she would still be younger than any recognized European writer, and yet her fame, which is already considerable, has been entirely posthumous.'

IX

PANDITA RAMABAI

WOMEN'S CHAMPION

If there are such few accounts of Indian travellers to the west, from women there are even fewer. There are records that the Mughal queens made the pilgrimage to Mecca, as did noble women later. Poor women from poverty-stricken families travelled out as indentured labour to the sugar plantations in the West Indies and to places like Fiji and Mauritius, but we do not know much of their stories first-hand.

It was from the 1870s onwards that well-known Indian women of the 19th century, such as Toru Dutt, then Ramabai, Cornelia Sorabji, Rakhmabai, Sarojini Naidu, and others travelled westward. They went to study and also to seek support for their reform programmes. These women worked for the education of women and to arouse awareness on their condition.

One such reformer and far-thinking educationist was Pandita Ramabai, who lived between 1858 and 1922. An educator and social reformer, she first visited England in 1883. Later, she also travelled to the US in 1886. Even before this, she had earned great fame in India for her extensive knowledge of the sacred texts, her passionate devotion to the cause of educational and social reform for women and girls, and her constant questioning of tradition.

CHILDHOOD WANDERER

Ramabai faced tragedy early on in her life. Her parents, Ananta and Lakshmibai Dongre, and a sister perished in the terrible famine of 1876–77 that affected a large part of western India. She wrote about her parents and her experience of this famine in a book called *Famine Experiences*.

Her family was learned and scholarly but had fallen into poverty. It was then that they took up a life of wandering. They moved from place to place as Puranikas, or narrators of sacred stories from the Puranas.

The family's wanderings began when Ramabai was only six months old. Her mother recounted to her how she had been placed as a baby in a cane box and carried around from place to place. But they had not been trained in any manual skill at all. This left them at the mercy of the famine when most people had nothing to give away and their reading of the sacred texts, in a time of all-round misery, found no takers at all.

Ramabai's father had always encouraged her mother Lakshmibai to learn to read, and so Lakshmibai became well versed in the Puranas and other sacred texts. But her mother's literacy made her father unpopular for a time. The conservatives believed that women, being of a lower status than men, should not read the sacred texts. Ananta Dongre's knowledge of the sacred texts enabled him to defend his decision to teach his wife Sanskrit, 'the sacred language of the gods.' Ramabai too learned Sanskrit from her mother. For their devotion to learning, Ramabai held her parents in high regard.

A SCHOLAR WHO QUESTIONED TRADITION

After Ramabai lost her parents and sister to the famine, she, together with her brother, Shrinivas, became a 'famine wanderer'. At this point, she began to question faith and caste rules that dictated life. The siblings travelled everywhere, covering much of the country on foot. They went as far north as Kashmir and then moved east to Calcutta in 1878. It was here that Ramabai and her brother first came into contact with Christianity, a relatively new religion in these parts, and one practised by the British and the Portuguese in the city of Calcutta.

Ramabai spent much of her time in Calcutta, studying books of Hindu law, especially the Dharma Shastras, and the

Mahabharata. Her learning and oratorical skills impressed many. Calcutta was not as narrow-minded as other places then in India. Ramabai was asked by pundits and other learned people in the city to speak to women in *purdah*, or those who lived secluded lives, on the duties of women according to the Shastras (sacred texts).

However, Ramabai continued to constantly question tradition and even the sacred texts. She knew women were considered inferior beings and it was believed that unless a woman subdued her will and being to that of her husband's, she was denied salvation or *moksha*. Women were not allowed to study the most important Sanskrit texts, i.e., the Vedas and Vedanta (texts associated with the Vedas).

Ramabai herself had been reluctant to read the Vedas at first but had been persuaded by Keshub Chandra Sen, a leading reformer in Calcutta, to read these texts. A growing awareness made her believe that the Shastras and other texts she read imposed no such sanctions on women reading them. Her travels also made her see first-hand the miserable conditions in which many women, especially those poor and widowed, lived. She realized that two things needed immediate attention: women's education and their health.

By this time, she was not just a Sanskrit scholar but well versed in a number of other languages too. She knew quite a bit of English as well. She was 20 and was referred to as 'Pandita,' denoting an eminent scholar-teacher. One of the other names she was referred to by was 'Sarasvati,' with reference to the Hindu goddess of learning.

Unfortunately, she soon lost her brother Shrinivas to an illness. In 1880, she married a Bengali gentleman of a different caste. Since this was an inter-caste marriage, it made the conservatives angry. She had to marry according to civil laws. Ramabai's husband, Bipin Behari Das, worked as a lawyer in the court at Sylhet, in Bengal.

The very vocal opposition to her marriage, and the criticism that came her way for marrying 'late' at 22, were things she wrote about in her book, *The High-Caste Hindu Woman*, where she blamed the Hindu marriage system and the system of caste for the low status and condition of girls and women in India. When her husband died of cholera a year later in 1881, Ramabai, with her year-old daughter Manorama, returned to Poona (now Pune).

WOMEN IN THE 19TH CENTURY

In Poona, Ramabai's lectures on the condition of women had a great impact on members of the upper classes and educated families, who attended them. She was able to set up the Arya Mahila Samaj devoted to the education of girls. She also spoke up for the postponement of marriage till the girl attained a certain mature age. Encouraged by the success of this project in Poona, she travelled to other cities in the Bombay Presidency, forming branches of the Arya Mahila Samaj, wherever she went.

She came to attention again in 1882 when she spoke before a government commission called the Hunter Commission. It had been set up to look into the condition of women in India and make recommendations to the British Raj to take steps by way of reform or action.

Ramabai angered many male reformers by mentioning that 99 per cent of Indian men were opposed to women's education. Ramabai believed that women should be instructed before marriage in Sanskrit and the vernacular (regional language). She also condemned the practice of child marriage. Ramabai told the Commission that for education to thrive, women themselves had to be trained as teachers. She also spoke of the need to have 'lady doctors' in India as women often refused to be attended to by male doctors.

Her thoughts about the condition of Indian women were shared by a growing number of social reformers, such as Mahadev Govind Ranade who had set up the Prarthana Samaj to work for women's education and widow remarriage. In that same period, Tarabai Shinde, a reformer concerned about women's education and their legal rights, wrote a pamphlet, *A Comparison between Men and Women*, which made a scathing criticism of how the genders were made unequal in every way. Then there was the famous Rakhmabai case that raised a controversy in the mid-1880s.

This was after Rakhmabai, a young woman, refused to move into her husband's home, despite having been married to him as a child bride. The case divided conservatives and reformers, many of whom were against the court's intervention in Indian 'tradition', but it highlighted the question of early marriage and women's rights.

TRAVEL FOR A CAUSE

Ramabai decided to travel to England in 1883. She went to the west at a time when travel by high-caste Hindu women was considered heretical, a break with tradition.

Ramabai was motivated by the issue of women's rights in India and wanted to raise awareness on the matter. But mainly, her desire was to start a school that would train girls to become future teachers, and for this, she needed to train herself first.

It was the missionaries she had come across during her work in Poona, the Sisters of the Community of Saint Mary the Virgin (CSMV), who made arrangements for Ramabai, a companion Anandibai Bhagat and Ramabai's daughter Manorama, to travel to England. They were to stay at Wantage, the headquarters of the CSMV at Oxfordshire in south England. This group was active all over England and Europe, running schools, mission houses (homes for the poor), and homes for the elderly, mothers and infants.

Ramabai sought support but was always wary of accepting charity. She was independent, questioning and assertive. She decided to write a book in Marathi, *Stree Dharma-Neeti* (Sacred Traditions of Women), which was published in 1883. The proceeds from its sale financed her passage to England. She also came to Britain on the understanding that she would teach Marathi to the Sisters at Wantage in return for being taught English, and for her and her companions' room and board. This independence led her to question western theology as well.

In England, she met Dorothea Beale, the well-known educator. This meeting enabled her to study at the Cheltenham Ladies' College. Women's higher education even in the west had comparatively late beginnings. Beale was an educational reformer, a reputed author and also the principal of Cheltenham Ladies' College, which was founded in 1853. Beale was also a suffragist - a believer that women should have the right to vote, which so far was disallowed even in the west. Ramabai studied in this college for some time and also taught Sanskrit there.

After this, she decided to leave for America at the invitation of Rachel Bodley, dean of the women's medical college in Pennsylvania (the first women's medical college ever).

A JOURNEY TO THE AMERICA

In 1885, Dr Rachel Bodley had written to Ramabai, inviting her to the graduation ceremony in which India's first woman doctor, Anandibai Gopal Joshi, was to graduate.

As Ramabai made up her mind to travel to the United States in 1886, she wrote what became her most famous book in the West, *The High-Caste Hindu Woman*. Ramabai dedicated her book to both Rachel Bodley and Anandibai Joshi. She wrote the book especially to pay for her own expenses. Even before she left for America, ten thousand copies of her book had been sold and Ramabai earned a sum of twenty-five thousand rupees.

Ramabai sailed for America from Liverpool, with her daughter Manorama, in a ship called the Sea *Princess*. In the third-class were some 190 other passengers, many of them new immigrants to America. As the ship neared the American coast, they encountered severe bad weather. This was in the area popularly called the 'Devil's Pot' in the north Atlantic, east of the coast of Newfoundland in Canada. The ship weathered the gale, but a few days later, it was stuck in ice in Delaware River, a river in north-eastern US that led to the main port. The ship remained stuck thus for some days. It took four or five smaller ships to dredge the ice before the *Sea Princess* could move safely to harbour.

UNFULFILLED DREAMS

Ramabai had planned to visit the US for a month, but she ended up staying for three years. The graduation ceremony during which she witnessed Anandibai Joshi being awarded her degree moved her deeply.

It was Rachel Bodley who first arranged for a reception in Ramabai's honour in the Young Men's Christian Association building in Philadelphia. It was attended by a select company of local women and Ramabai spoke to the gathering on 'The Women of India.' It was her first public address before an American audience, and they were deeply impressed by her words.

A newspaper report of the time described the reception in these terms:

'The address delivered by Pundita Ramabai was unwritten. Standing in an easy attitude, with her hands clasped upon the desk before her, and speaking with a voice of the most musical sweetness and distinctness, and with the unembarrassed manner of a genuine simplicity, she told the story of Hindu womanhood to her American audience in a fashion that won all hearts and riveted all attention.'

Ramabai soon became popular in the US. She gave numerous lectures on women's issues and the need for women's education in various cities around north-east and mid-west US. She even ventured further out west, reaching as far as Denver in Colorado, where she was most impressed by the Rocky Mountains. Most of her addresses to the public were based on what she had written about in her book, *The High-Caste Hindu Woman.*

Having travelled around in Britain and now in the US, she had a much clearer idea of what she wanted to do on her return to India. Besides educating and training teachers, Ramabai's mission became to raise money for the school she wanted to start back in India – and here she was remarkably successful. The public school system of America that included girls as well as boys, and its kindergarten system – that ensured motor learning as well as mental skills – greatly attracted Ramabai. Ramabai's hope was to establish an educational home for young widows, 'who in their turn would go forth as teachers to enlighten the darkness of their countrywomen'. She enrolled herself for a course in kindergarten studies in a Philadelphia training school.

Rachel Bodley, who wrote the preface to Ramabai's book *The High-Caste Hindu Woman*, wrote about the life and early death of Anandibai Joshi, who tragically died in early 1887, only months after returning to India. Bodley also detailed Ramabai's own life story and wrote in support of Ramabai's appeal for help.

In order to help her raise the funds necessary for starting and sustaining the work she dreamt of, her friends and associates set about organizing 'Ramabai Circles' in different places. Her supporters promised to give a fixed sum of money annually over 10 years. These support circles transmitted their contributions to the trustees of an association called the 'Ramabai Association', which was formed in 1887 at Boston's Channing Hall.

The reception she received in the US amazed and touched Ramabai. Not surprisingly, then, on her return she wrote a detailed account of the US, its history, its customs and its people. This book, written in Marathi, was called *Peoples of the United States* and was later translated into English as well.

TALKING ABOUT THE US

In the book, though Ramabai was effusive and enthusiastic about the progress the US had made in several areas, she also criticized the country's problems with race issues, its persecution of the Native Americans (American Indians), and of course, the resistance to women's emancipation.

While she was notably impressed by the remarkable progress made with regard to women's education, for this was the time when enduring women's colleges were opening, and law and medical schools had seen their first women graduates, she was also taken aback and surprised by the resistance such measures still encountered.

She discussed books that added to the debate raging then on women's role in society. *Society in America* was a book written by an Englishwoman, Harriet Martineau, who had visited the US in 1834 and angrily criticized the state of women's education there. As Martineau wrote at the time, and Ramabai mentions these details, the education that American women aspired to was to enjoy a bit of singing, or to play a musical instrument, and engage in some reading, writing, and there was always needlework. They enjoyed little social and political freedom.

However, awareness grew by degrees all through the mid-19th century. For a long time, not a single high school for girls existed in Boston, the city that was Ramabai's base for the time she was in eastern US. It took 125 years after Harvard University was established, for colleges to be set up for women. In 1832, the Oberlin College was established and from 1834, it became the first institution of higher learning to open its doors to women.

Ramabai also mentioned books written by some feminists of the time, such as British feminist writer Mary Wollstonecraft's A *Vindication of the Rights of Women* in 1797. In this book, Wollstonecraft wrote with conviction that women were in no way an inferior species, but lack of education impeded their progress. Ramabai spoke eloquently of the early American feminists such as Emma

Hart Willard who lived between 1787 and 1870. Willard addressed the New York Senate in 1819 in her quest to set up a women's seminary. The Troy Female Seminary in Troy, New York, was the first school devoted to higher education for women.

After thoroughly presenting her cause and receiving not only sympathy but substantial help, Ramabai left America after being away for six years. In May 1888, Ramabai said farewell to her friends in Boston to travel to other cities and also to Canada. She travelled last to the Pacific Coast, making friends and forming 'Ramabai Circles' all along the way. In November that same year, she left America for India, this time sailing via San Francisco on the American west coast and reaching Hong Kong, after a long journey across the Pacific. On the way she did stop in China, but she didn't write much about this.

She arrived in Bombay on 1 February 1889, and it was here that that she began her life's work. Six weeks later, the Widows' Home was inaugurated in a house on Bombay's Chowpatty beach. It was called 'Sharada Sadan' (Abode of Wisdom). She remained for the rest of her life a champion of the women's cause and devoted herself to working for the welfare of women and girls. Later, she moved her base to Poona. Her reform work in western India was celebrated throughout the world. When she died in 1922, the *Times of India* referred to her as one of the 'makers of modern India.' The description remains true even to this day.

X

BEHRAMJI MALABARI

PILGRIM REFORMER

For some years before Behramji Malabari travelled to Britain in 1890, newspapers in India, along with reformers and the more educated classes, were fiercely debating the question of reform in Indian society, mainly relating to child marriage and widow remarriage. In 1884, Malabari, who was a journalist as well as a poet, published a set of 'notes' on infant marriage in India. He described the practice as a vicious 'social evil' that needed laws to stop it.

Then, in 1885, something sensational happened that made reform urgent.

That year the celebrated case of Rakhmabai filled the Bombay newspapers. Rakhmabai, a 22-year-old woman, refused to live in her husband's house and he filed a case in the court against Rakhmabai's decision. She had been married 11 years ago when she was just a child and had stayed separately from her 'husband'. Now she refused to move into his house, as tradition demanded. The initial court decision (in 1885) went in her favour, but her husband appealed for a review of the case, and the court ordered her to live with her husband or face an imprisonment term of six months. She refused and this gave more fillip to the agitation on the need to raise the 'Age of Consent', the age when girls could be lawfully married.

Malabari was born in Baroda, now a city in Gujarat that was then part of Bombay Presidency in 1853. He lost his father very young and was adopted by a trader whose business interests were in the Malabar region (in present-day Kerala) and Behramji took his guardian's name. He was proficient in both Gujarati and English. His second book of poems, written in English, following the first written in Gujarati, won considerable acclaim when it was published in 1877. It was praised by people like Lord Alfred Tennyson and Florence Nightingale. Subsequently, he moved into journalism, roused by the issues and social concerns of the day.

Malabari's visit to Britain in 1890 was prompted by the need to win support among English reformers and politicians for laws that could improve the lot of Hindu child-wives and child-widows in India. His book, *The Indian Eye on English Life, or, Ramblings of a Pilgrim*

Reformer, however, mentions little of this as the reason for his travelling to Britain. Instead, Malabari begins by saying that by the end of 1889 he had travelled across most of the Indian continent and so what could be more natural for a 'student of humanity, a pilgrim in search of the truths of life, than that he should now wish for a look at the other world, beyond the seas'. The book is entertaining, filled with funny, keen observations as Malabari wandered the byways of London and travelled through Europe.

A FRIEND LIKE CROCODILE

He left on 1 April 1890, on board the steamship *Imperator*. With him was a friend, whom Malabari addressed as 'Crocodile' all through the book! He described Crocodile as someone who had been trained to do nothing in particular, who was, from childhood, used to a 'shabby-genteel' existence. Malabari had tried in vain to shape him into a useful member of society, but Crocodile tired of a settled life soon. He would break away under various pretexts – that he had a weak memory, or a short temper, and bad luck, especially. Crocodile gave himself airs that he was not born to be a servant, but then he could not even make a suitable master. Crocodile was a puzzle and a paradox. Malabari explained that the nickname suited him, for at the slightest excuse, he could cry like a crocodile, especially when the mistakes had been of his own making.

THE DREARY SUEZ

In the beginning it was such smooth sailing that many among Malabari's fellow passengers actually prayed for a gale and for all the stormy events at sea they had only read about. But these never did appear. In about two weeks, they reached Aden (Yemen) on the coast of Arabia, then a British settlement. Evidently, journeys by sea had become quicker; ships of a few decades ago had taken far longer.

Boys sailed up in small dugout canoes, and surrounded them, urging them to 'have a dive' in the sea. They came 'with shrill cries of aho-aho – heb a die (have a dive) aho, lard (lord) heb a die – leddy (lady), heb a die', and on hearing this, the passengers, if they were keen, threw coins of small denominations into the water. The boys dived into the water like flying fish, and came up again and again in the twinkling of an eye, holding the tiny little coins high between their fingers.

Aden had thrived since the advent of British rule. A veritable desert, it now had roads, tunnels and water tanks. There were trees planted on the roadsides.

The Suez Canal was a splendid piece of work, but their passage through it appeared dreadfully slow to Malabari. It was so monotonous that it reminded Malabari of the truth of the idiom, 'dull as ditchwater'. The arid desert on both sides, the sand heaped up on the banks, the flies that infested the place, all heightened the desolate look of the place. The wild and strange-looking country beyond interested him more than the much admired feat of engineering before him.

Port Said seemed an undesirable place to disembark but Malabari was obliged to go ashore for a bit, in order to escape the storm of coal-dust and the babble of incoherent sounds at the port. In the main street there were shops offering coffee, cigars, tobacco, sweets and cheap curiosities. At the very end of the street was a large cafe with a music hall, and on noting their entry, the proprietor clapped his hands in welcome. This was a signal for the orchestra to begin playing. Malabari and his group from the ship enjoyed the ginger ale they were served and the music too was not bad.

A BIT OF EUROPE

Sailing across the Mediterranean, their first port of call was Brindisi in southern Italy. It was a welcome sight to the eye tired of gazing on deserts and an endless expanse of water. The harbour was one of the prettiest. As they moved along the Italian coast, and reached Trieste, in north-western Italy, Malabari felt the town looked much like Bombay then. He noted the women, barefoot and in simple calico dresses, carrying baskets of bread, eggs, fruits and vegetables.

In Venice, it thrilled him to see men and women enjoying themselves in gondolas in the limpid moonlight, singing under the archways. Malabari and a few others walked everywhere, helped by a sharp young guide. In fact, some of them wore off the soles of their shoes with all the walking!

In Switzerland, to the north of Italy, they travelled through St. Gothard's Tunnel, which was a stupendous work of engineering. Malabari found the views around magnificent. It took him some time to realize that the white substance by the roadside was snow and not cotton as he had first surmised. He wrote that the entire roadway was covered by a 'carpet of *pasham*' (flakes of wool).

THE CROWDED STREETS OF LONDON

In those days, in the late 19th century, trains through Europe ran to Paris and then Calais on the French coast. From here, passengers took the ferry across the English Channel to Dover, which was on the south-east coast of England. Malabari found the drive from Dover to London very pleasant.

At Victoria Station, he was struck by the noise and bustle around him. The traffic was heavier than he had ever seen in India during its annual fairs and more than in any European city he had seen so far. It was all due to 'railway trains, running underground and above ground . . . omnibuses, trams, cabs, private carriages, wagons, trucks, hand-barrows, tricycles, etc., to say nothing of the immense pedestrian crowds.' He noted the 'boy-sweepers' who ran about between carriages, and even under them, in order to keep the ground clean. They were as agile as mice or squirrels.

He made amusing observations about the crowds, noticing that simply everybody appeared to be out of breath for they walked too fast. He wondered if this 'rapid locomotion' was a matter of habit or simply because the cold weather made them want to hurry. This constant rush left them with little time for conversation with anyone else.

THE STRANGE WEATHER

He found the weather in Britain capricious. It could rain without warning. He had never seen an entire day in London that he could honestly describe as absolutely 'fine'. One could speak of a 'fine' five minutes, or even a fine half-hour or hour, but nothing beyond that.

He went to the usual places, all described with eloquence by travellers who had preceded him. These included the Westminster Abbey, the Houses of Parliament, St. Paul's Cathedral, the Crystal Palace, Hampton Court, the South Kensington Museum of Natural History, the Art Gallery, the British Museum, Madame Tussaud's Exhibition and the Zoological Gardens.

The average street of London presented a very monotonous look, unrelieved by a variety of construction or colour. The parks, however, were the pride and glory of London. These were extensive, wonderfully well kept and easy to access. On his walks through London, Malabari was accosted by the street urchins who would mock and jeer at his foreign attire. Sometimes, he admitted, he was overdressed for the occasion. Well-meaning English ladies also walked up to him, wanting to take his photograph as if he were an exotic species.

HOW ENGLISH FAMILIES LIVED

During his stay in London, Malabari lived in a number of different arrangements but preferred 'the boarding-house' to most other options.

He had high praise for his landlady, who appears in his book as 'Mrs M-.' Mrs M's second husband was a florist and she had children – ranging from four to 40 years old – from two marriages. Annie, her daughter, 'was a quiet, self-contained little lady, with a very fine devotional nature (and) fond of music'. Malabari also mentioned Maggie, Mrs M's 'maid-of-all-work.' He mentioned how, 'it was a sight to see her heaving up, like a steam engine, with broom and mop and duster.'

Malabari wrote in passing that shortly after Maggie left to get married, he and Crocodile also moved out. He hinted that their departure was prompted by the fact that Mrs M did not approve of Crocodile, who ate more than she felt Malabari was paying for.

However, he was still full of praise for Mrs M, seeing in her 'the English mother' who was the centre of the British domestic empire, as he saw it. The success of English civilization was to be found, Malabari argued, in their system of matrimony, and the equality between husband and wife. Malabari's tone was not at all contemptuous of tradition, but he did want his readers to be aware of the reforms that Indian society needed, especially in how its women were treated.

THE POOR OF LONDON

In London, he wrote about the hundreds of people who faced a daily, almost hourly, struggle to keep body and soul together. The poverty of England appeared at its worst during winter that usually lasted six straight months.

Many men and women, who were perhaps disabled by accident or had been thrown out of work, trudged aimlessly about, not knowing where to get a crust of bread, or even a 'dry bone' to allay the 'hunger that gnawed away at their vitals'. Malabari wrote about seeing many such people lying on the pavements, by the roadside, sometimes even on house stoops, looking starved and emaciated. He appreciated the involvement of aristocratic and middle-class English women in charity. He described how they were often seen in the streets, walking, even marching in groups, distributing clothes and food to the poor.

LONDON'S FAMILIAR FIGURES

Still immersed in his description of London street life, Malabari wrote that the policeman was trusted and feared equally. He described the different kinds of knocks the postman had. Depending on the packages he had to deliver – a registered letter, or a parcel, for instance – he would deliver either a cheery tap on the door, or else a series of these. The telegraph boy, on the other hand, reminded him of the Roman god Mercury, for he appeared to rush everywhere on winged feet.

One of the saddest sights Malabari recounts having seen in the London was that of the organ-grinder. He recounted the one he saw, who looked like an Italian. There were a couple of caged birds over her instrument and she played it, standing akimbo. She hoped passers-by would reward her with a few coins but her expression never gave anything away: neither sorrow nor joy. The streets offered an immense variety of vocal music too. An old tramp produced some magically sweet music by making his fingers run over glasses, some empty, others filled with water in varying quantities.

THE PARLIAMENT AND INSINCERE PEOPLE

On one occasion he attended the debate on the Indian budget in the British House of Commons. Malabari arrived too late to hear the eminent Indian liberal Dadabhai Naoroji speak. But he was disappointed: The 'thinness of attendance, and the indifference of the few that are present' in the Parliament chilled him.

He was also critical of the English government in his book, hoping they would pay more attention to Indian affairs. Many among the English, Malabari wrote, had a patronizing attitude towards those in the colonies. In one lengthy passage, he upbraided an unnamed English Member of Parliament for failing to be courteous to him.

Malabari made several unsuccessful attempts to meet with this parliamentarian (he only describes him in the book as 'a prominent nobleman'). Malabari finally gained a private hearing to speak to him about his proposals for reforming child marriage laws. But, all through their meeting, Malabari wrote, the Member of Parliament sat there talking, 'smoking, and glancing at letters just brought in.'

Malabari was not able to extract a promise of public support for his reform project from the parliamentarian as the meeting came to a close. Later, Malabari had to write reminders to him every week, till he obtained some kind of commitment from the London committee then deliberating this matter. Indeed, the matter came up for debate in the British Parliament. It was in March 1891 that the Government of British India enacted the Age of Consent Act that raised the age of consent (and thus, marriage) for all girls, from 10 to 12 years.

He moved on to speak about the most sought-after occupations of the time. The military and a career in Parliament were greatly preferred, so was a term of service in India, especially as an officer of the Imperial Civil Service and in the British Indian Army. A military career in India was a prized opportunity for sons from noble families. It was very handsomely paid, and offered immense prospects of 'power and preferment.'

THE WONDER OF THE RAILWAYS

Like the travellers before him, Malabari was amazed by the railways. He described the railroads as among London's most familiar sights, just 'as the whistle of the engine is the most frequent sound.' The passenger traffic was enormous and there were more trains in England than in India, which was several times bigger and had a much larger population.

He emphasized the startling difference of behaviour between authorities and officials in England and those he had encountered in India. For instance, the guards and other junior railway officials he encountered in London were a contrast to the railway men in India. The former were always courteous when they addressed people: 'Yes, sir; no, ma'am, yes, lady.' The railway carriages too were more comfortable than in India.

For really enjoyable travelling, Malabari wrote that he missed the journeys he had undertaken in a bullock cart. They would set off at the crack of dawn, and stop only after six hours or so for a necessary halt for rest and food. It was a pleasant experience, with conversation between the traveller and the driver, and even the bullocks, with their ponderous gait and frequent nodding of head, appeared participants in this.

TRAVELS THROUGH EUROPEAN CITIES

Malabari left for Paris in September 1890, accompanied by a friend who promised to show him the sights. He saw people dining out in the streets. Of the many places he visited, he recalled especially the Galleries and the tomb of Napoleon, a splendid work of art, representing the emperor in his full lost glory. The visit made him philosophical as he questioned Napoleon's rise to fame and his equally swift fall.

At Cologne in Germany, he had the hottest and the

noisiest tram ride in his memory. The heat was worth comparing to that of Bombay and yet the people appeared to work heartily. Once they had entered the province of Bavaria in southeast Germany, they passed through fine countryside that looked 'remarkably like India in the habits of the people and their way of ploughing.'

Munich was an interesting old town, with large broad streets, clean and well-swept, spacious roads, and paved sidewalks just as wide as the roads of Bombay. The Austrian countryside looked fertile, studded as it was with valleys and lakes. When he saw crows here, his first glimpse of them in Europe, he was instantly reminded of home. The snow-capped hills of the Alps delighted him and reminded him of the Ghats that ran along the western length of Bombay Presidency (now Maharashtra). The scene was one of 'rugged magnificence'.

He also wrote of a fine day spent in Oberammergau, Bavaria. He had driven up with a friend to King Ludwig II's palace (Ludwig had been ruler of Bavaria till the mid-1880s and was a patron of the music composer Richard Wagner). They did part of the way on foot. They were exhausted but the magnificent scenery all around them more than made up for the effort. Malabari wrote that it made him forget Shimla and Mahabaleshwar, famous hill-stations of India.

ON TO ITALY

They entered Italy via Ala, in the very north of the country. The country appeared rich but flat, and it was already autumn. They travelled to Florence, then variously called the 'City of Flowers' and also the 'Flower of Cities.' He saw on his way a regular caravan of bullocks, goats and sheep, and was heartened to hear the familiar sound of their bells, as well as a shepherd singing a song. It made him even more nostalgic for home. The Picture Gallery at Florence was the best he had ever seen. Florence surpassed Paris and Munich in terms of the huge number of fine paintings displayed in its galleries.

From Florence, they headed off somewhat in a rush to Rome. The interior of St. Peter's in Rome looked 'grand and imposing, with its columns, domes, and paintings by old masters'. The Vatican, complete with its gardens, hospitals, colleges, the Pope's palace and his royal guards, was like a little kingdom in itself. From Rome they went on to Naples and then Venice, which this time he saw again at some leisure before boarding the ship at Trieste.

TINY BUT IMPORTANT BELGIUM

Malabari's second trip to England was later the next year in 1891. This time, he took the 'Brussels route' from Calais in France. Brussels, the capital of Belgium, held a peculiar interest for him as it was 'part French, part German, part English, and part, as it appears, American.' It had an air of freedom, of cleanliness and comfort, which he had not seen elsewhere. Here, for the first time, Malabari saw 'dogs yoked to little carts, and worked pretty much as horses and bullocks are worked in other countries.' Brussels had a large market, where both the buyers and sellers were almost all women, except the men who sold meat.

Antwerp in Belgium was one of the most ancient of seaport towns in Europe. At one time it traded with the whole of the then known world but had since fallen into decay. Antwerp had an old cathedral that displayed two masterpieces of the famous painter, Peter Paul Rubens.

They halted briefly at Frankfurt and Malabari wrote of being 'struck with the size and solidity of some of its buildings.' En route to Vienna, snow began falling again. Soon they were frozen inside their railway carriage, despite the service of hot air. He wrote of the poor conductor who had to walk in the bitter cold along the footboards. In those days, the footboards were placed outside the railway carriages. The conductor could hardly hold out his hand as he entered the carriage to punch their tickets, for he was freezing cold. Meanwhile, the train rushed on at breakneck speed through the dark hills.

Vienna had some stunning palatial buildings. It was one of Europe's cultural centres. Even private houses in the city were large and well built. The train from Vienna down south was somehow held up, and they had to catch another to Trieste in Italy where the steamer waited to take them back to Bombay. Malabari fretted about missing the steamer and was in a fever of anxiety. It was then that a German fellow passenger came to his rescue and they had a rushed adventure to get to Trieste in time.

The German, as Malabari described, was kind enough to get a carriage to drive him to the other station, and came along himself. It became a drive for dear life, with the coachman yelling and cracking his whip without pause. But when they arrived, the train was already in motion. He appealed desperately to the station-master, showering him with most of the silver (coins) he had. It was then that Malabari could make a blind rush for the train. The guard and another official hauled him up over the wheel of a ladies compartment, where his coat nearly got entangled. Everyone on the platform watched the proceedings with great interest. But he was hauled up at last, 'thanks partly to the help extended by a motherly occupant of the compartment.' His German friend tossed his ticket and the luggage in after Malabari and in return for his kindness, Malabari threw him 'a glance of unworded gratitude with a bundle of braided silk handkerchiefs I have carried in my breast pocket.'

He had another adventure just as the steamship neared Bombay. It was held up for a day near the docks but Malabari couldn't wait to get home. As a small dinghy approached, silently and stealthily, he jumped from board or was perhaps helped down (he doesn't elaborate). He thus reached home a full unofficial day in advance!

XI

CORNELIA SORABJI

LAWYER EXTRAORDINAIRE

Three years after Ramabai left for England in 1883, Cornelia Sorabji (1866–1954) too arrived there to study law at Somerville College, Oxford. She was the first Indian woman to do so, and she had several other firsts to her credit as well. She was the first woman graduate of Bombay University and only one of four first-class degree holders when she graduated.

She was also the first lawyer to appear in an Indian court (the Allahabad High Court). But all such successes did not come easily to her. Yet, in her writings about herself and in her fiction too, she does not come across as an embittered woman.

A REFORMIST HOUSEHOLD

Cornelia came from a progressive family. Her mother founded four schools, all in the house where they lived in Pune. Two of these, in fact, came up in the garden of the house. Her mother was Francina Ford, an Indian who had been adopted by a British couple. She firmly believed in not discriminating against anyone on the basis of religion, caste or gender. In the first of her memoirs that Cornelia Sorabji wrote in 1934, called *India Calling*, she is full of praise of her mother and acknowledges her mother's influence on her life. Cornelia's sister Susie too studied medicine abroad and became a pioneering woman doctor.

Cornelia's father, who believed firmly in women's education, tried very hard to get Cornelia's two older sisters into Bombay University, but they were refused; thus far no woman had ever been to university.

GETTING TO OXFORD, ONE WAY OR ANOTHER

Cornelia still became the first woman to secure admission as a student of Bombay University. She matriculated at the age of 16 (at this time, such exams were conducted by the university). Six years later, she also stood first in her college in English Literature; hers was also one of the four first-class degrees that year. She managed this despite all the obstacles that came her way – boys even slammed the lecture-room doors in her face, trying to prevent her from attending them.

She then hoped to secure a scholarship to travel to England, to continue her studies. But the scholarship was again refused on the grounds that she was a woman. This matter about a woman being refused a scholarship because of her gender was reported in the newspapers and came up for discussion in Britain's House of Commons.

Following this, some eminent British women, including Florence Nightingale who had revolutionized the field of nursing in the 1850s and was widely known as the 'Lady with the Lamp', got together and among themselves, collected the amount required to get Cornelia a scholarship. When Cornelia travelled to Oxford in England in 1889, it was the first time a woman from India was doing so.

Cornelia arrived to study in Somerville College, set up around a decade before. The first head of Somerville, Madeleine Shaw-Lefevre, had supported Cornelia's coming to Somerville, for she had known about the schools her mother had set up and admired this initiative. Somerville had been named in honour of the Scottish mathematician and scientist Mary Somerville (1780–1872), who had been largely self-taught.

In London, Cornelia Sorabji came into contact with some of the great minds of her time, including the eminent jurist, A.V. Dicey, the scholar and linguist Max Müller, and the philosopher Benjamin Jowett, who was to be her mentor.

Despite the opposition that continued to come her way first in her academic life and later professionally, she passed the Bachelor of Civil Law exam in 1892. She could really only qualify for the bar in 1922 (owing to legal constraints on women at the time).

STUDYING AT OXFORD

When Cornelia arrived, she was told that as she was a woman (again!), she could only read English Literature, for law was not an option open to women. No woman in even in Britain had enrolled for such a degree.

It was the Master of Balliol College, the philosopher Benjamin Jowett, who spoke up for her. This position was a unique and highly respected one; a person who commanded the respect of his peers was usually chosen as Master. Not only did Jowett encourage her pursuit of scholarship, he also introduced her to several leading figures of Victorian society. Once he even sent her to meet Florence Nightingale, who had been one of her benefactors.

Jowett had a special Law course devised solely for her, as women were not allowed formally to study law. Cornelia attended specific lectures in Law, especially those by Sir William Markby, whose lectures were attended by both senior and junior Indian Civil Service men who had come up to Oxford. She also attended Professor Bryce's lectures on the philosophy of law and how the legal system had developed over the centuries. Eventually, it was Jowett who arranged things such that she could appear for the examination for the degree of Bachelor of Civil Law.

Just before the exam, however, one of the examiners refused to examine her – again on the grounds that she was a woman and that there was no precedent. So Benjamin Jowett summoned the Oxford's University Council to debate the motion that Oxford University should accept Cornelia Sorabji, and it was passed. But the examiner remained unfazed and gave her a much lower division than she had hoped for – a third, and this really upset her. She had passed, though she would collect the degree only 30 years later in 1922.

At special weekend parties, Jowett also introduced her to the cream of London society. It was here that she met politicians, and present and future prime ministers such as William Gladstone and Arthur Balfour, and the brothers Alfred and Neville Lyttelton who were in politics and sports. She met another future prime minister H. Asquith and his wife Margot Tennant. Besides, there were judges, eminent jurists, philosophers and linguists, writers, historians and essayists. She met two well-known novelists of the time, Mrs Humphrey Ward and Miss Braddon, others like Lady Stanley of Alderley who was a campaigner for women's education in England, and Henry Morton Stanley – the famous explorer in Africa.

She wrote that she learnt things of immense value from all she met. She understood, from following developments in England's politics, that freedom of thought was just as important as freedom of religion. What was of special importance to her was the realization that freedom of opinion and even disagreement did not come in the way of friendship with anyone.

Her younger brother Richard soon followed her to Oxford and she found his company delightful. She enjoyed boating on the river Cherwell that ran by Oxford and was soon an expert rower. One summer vacation, accompanied by her brother and friends, she went down the river in a dinghy one of the friends owned, as far as Richmond in London. She came to love the river Thames as well, and described it eloquently in her book, *India Calling*.

MEETING THE QUEEN AND POETS

She was also very thrilled when she was formally presented at court before the queen: 'Queen Victoria sent me a gracious message to the effect that "one of my pretty colours" would be permitted': and I wore an azalea sari, something in colour between pink and yellow. The Queen said she was "glad to see me there" when she gave me her hand to kiss, and the long sequence of curtseys ended (we did several, in those days, slithering past bunches of Serene Highnesses) . . .'

Cornelia also has a memorable meeting with the famous playwright George Bernard Shaw. He evidently knew of the opposition to British rule that was growing at that time in India (late 1880s). This perhaps explains why he greeted Cornelia by asking her why she was not in prison. Yet Cornelia found him kind and gentle, and described him as being full of humour.

It was Jowett who arranged for Cornelia and Richard to meet the poet Lord Alfred Tennyson, in his last days. Tennyson read to them his last poem about Akbar the Great, for he wanted the two young Indians to advise him about whether he had made any mistakes. It was only shortly afterwards that Cornelia was asked to the moving funeral service for Tennyson held in Westminster Abbey, where 'Crossing the Bar,' one of Tennyson's most famous poems, was read out.

HER LEGAL CAREER

Cornelia spent a year in London with a solicitors' firm. She was allowed to read in the library in Lincoln's Inn, where the most prominent legal firms had their offices, and in another first, she was perhaps the first woman allowed to read here. When she returned to Bombay in 1894, the Chief Justice in Bombay told the solicitors who had first invited her not to employ a woman, so the job she had been offered was taken back. She again passed the Bachelor of Law exam in Bombay University in 1897 and also the pleader's exam in Allahabad in 1899 but to no avail. She could not practise as a lawyer nor appear in court. The law that barred women from practising law was repealed only in 1924.

She then found that, although the British were not prepared to have a woman as a lawyer in Bombay, the maharajas or rulers of the princely states were more than happy to have her. For the next five years she worked at making a career for herself in law, attempting to be a barrister and working for these princes.

However, only the most frivolous cases came her way. There was one instance she writes about in *India Calling*, when she had to decide if an elephant was guilty of rampaging through a maharaja's banana grove. In the end, the case was dismissed and the elephant pronounced 'not guilty' because the maharaja, who had first complained about the animal, turned out to be the judge as well.

THE WOMEN IN SECLUSION

In 1899, the condition of the secluded upper-class women called the *purdanashin* (meaning 'behind veil or curtain') women came to her attention. Some of these (behind veil or curtain) had been child brides. Once married, many never saw the outside world again. They could not speak to any man other than their husband; and once widowed, they could not speak to any man at all. They were ignorant of the law, but they were wealthy and owned land and jewellery of great value. As widows, they also served as guardians for their male heirs, holding charge of huge estates that they had a 'right to use' as long as the heirs were alive. However, because they had little legal help, often such women were cheated out of such property, especially in cases where the heirs were too young. Sorabji knew they faced problems of traditional rules, and helplessness regarding people who swindled them out of their wealth by fraud, and in some instances, by murdering their children.

Cornelia worked at persuading the British government in favour of a legal representative who could help such women, but it was an uphill task. In 1902, the question was raised in Britain's House of Commons again about whether the Government was doing anything to provide for the needs of these women. It was only in 1904, five years after Sorabji took up their cause, that the Secretary of State for India agreed to such a position for Sorabji. She was appointed Lady Assistant to the court of wards. It would be her responsibility to act as legal adviser to the *purdanashin* women. She remained in this position for 18 years and was indispensable to the women she represented and worked for.

Her nephew, also called Richard like her brother, wrote a book on her where he describes how 'she was carried to these fabulous palaces on a palanquin through the middle of the jungle.' She did more than just safeguard the legal rights of these women. She brought about reconciliations between families when legal cases were too expensive. She even looked after their health for such women rarely consulted doctors or received good medical care. Sometimes she appointed tutors, both for young girls and boys, to ensure that even they knew their rights and how to manage their estates.

TRAVELLING DURING A WAR

Cornelia made a visit to England in 1914, just before the First World War broke out. This trip was memorable because she met the illustrator Edmund Dulac, who would collaborate with her on her book for children called *Sun Babies*.

Sorabji wrote in *India Calling* that she decided to visit London again in 1918, when the war was still on, for her eyes had now begun giving her trouble. She wrote that by the end of 1918, she was afraid of going blind as she 'overused' her eyes so much. It was perhaps a kind of glaucoma, but medical knowledge of the time did not allow for its early detection. Since it was wartime, travelling across the seas and even between countries was difficult. Her doctor feared the long journey would prove perilous, but the then Viceroy, Lord Chelmsford, gave her special permission to travel through the Canal.

Sorabji wrote that it was a thrilling voyage where their passenger ship was 'camouflaged' to carry soldiers and provisions. From Port Said the ship was part of a convoy of 21 ships, and the entire line moved in a zigzag way every time danger threatened or there were torpedoes feared underwater. They had orders to always have lifebelts on in case the ship sank suddenly, and to 'wear our heaviest coats when called to the (life) boats.' The question 'what shall I save?' often confronted them. Sorabji had with her a miniature portrait of her mother and it sat perfectly in her shirt pocket. The news of peace having been declared only came to her once the ship was nearing London. Sorabji's eyes were saved by her English doctor, and at the end of six months she was back again at work in India.

She returned to London in 1922, to collect her Bar degree. It was the year women were called to the Bar, and the very next year, Sorabji too returned to practise law in Calcutta.

As a lawyer, like many 'moderate' Indian nationalists, she did not believe in the civil disobedience that Mahatma Gandhi popularized. She believed, like the 'moderate Congressmen' before her, that India must seek independence by legal and constitutional means. When in London, she wrote letters to *The Times* on laws that were being debated and, on Indian self-governance. She also met Gandhi once, when both tried to argue each other out of their convictions.

TELLING AMERICANS ABOUT BRITISH INDIA

In the autumn of 1929, Sorabji received a cable from America. She had been invited by the Institute of Politics at Williamstown in Massachusetts to join in the discussions on India.

She wrote that she had never wanted to go to America but came away 'loving it, and loving the American people.' She found them 'fair-minded', but with regard to British India, they had never had a proper chance to form their judgements. Sorabji was conservative in her political beliefs; she was also an 'Anglophile', an admirer of British systems for in her early days. She had learnt much in London and had received generous help from many people she had known there.

After her session at Williamstown, she accepted invitations to speak in several other American States, so as to discuss the Indian situation in public. All through the winter of 1930–31, she toured both the east and west coasts of America, as part of her speaking engagements. She visited Canada too and received much kindness from the Canadians, in part because the people she met and interacted with in Ottawa had been friends of her sister Susie. Susie, as a doctor, had travelled extensively in America and Canada.

SAVING HER EYES JUST IN TIME

It was in America that her eyes began to fail her again and she consulted a famous eye surgeon based in Baltimore, Maryland. He operated on her at short notice but warned her that there was every danger of her losing her sight soon. Back in London, even the doctor who had 'saved' her eyes in 1918 informed her that no doctor could do anything for her now, but Sorabji was cheerful: 'I thanked God that I was in a country where I could at least learn to be blind.' Things she had taken for granted such as the faces of little children and of friends, now appeared doubly sweeter and precious.

When she returned to the specialist in a month's time, he informed her that the reason for her failing eyesight had been found: it was rheumatism, till now wrongly treated as glaucoma. Now, he sent her to another specialist. It was a miracle as her sight did improve marginally and served her sufficiently for her needs in later years. Yet her deteriorating health prompted a permanent move to England in the 1930s. Here, she became a writer, penning her two memoirs and several other books, including a play called *Gold Mohur*. She died in 1954. Much later, a bust of her was unveiled in 2012 at Lincoln's Inn, London.

XII

SWAMI VIVEKANANDA

MONK AND REFORMER

Swami Vivekananda (1863–1902), born Narendra Nath Datta, was a monk, a famous disciple of Sri Ramakrishna, the noted spiritual teacher in Bengal, and he was also a dedicated social reformer. He travelled widely in the United States, Europe and Asia. During this time, most Indians saw themselves as people of a nation subject to British domination, but Vivekananda believed India was no decaying nation. Instead, he believed efforts had to be made to rejuvenate and regenerate India. His travels were journeys to learn, discover and promote understanding between regions and religions.

On his return from his first successful visit to the US in 1895, he told a journalist that his reasons for going to

America were many, but in short he had decided to go west once he had walked all over India and seen most of it. In the early 1890s, during the course of his wanderings and spiritual search through India, he had heard about the Parliament of Religions in Chicago and was keen to spread India's message there. Ajit Singh, the Raja of Khetri, the ruler of a principality now in Rajasthan, arranged for his travel. It was the raja who provided him with a robe of orange silk, a turban of the same colour, a first-class ticket on a ship called the *S.S. Peninsular* as also the necessary wherewithal to cover Vivekananda's initial expenses there. The ship sailed from Bombay on 31 May 1893, and reached America more than a month later. It was the same raja who bestowed on him the name 'Vivekananda' meaning 'one who receives joy in knowledge and reasoning'. It was this name by which he was to become famous. Some of Vivekananda's travel accounts appear in his letters to his disciples or family in Calcutta.

ASIA AND ITS SPIRITUAL UNITY

In one of his first letters, Vivekananda wrote that life on a ship was very different from that of a wandering monk, but he soon adjusted himself to it. His orange robe aroused the curiosity of many fellow passengers, who were soon impressed by his serious nature and scholarship. Vivekananda enjoyed the voyage, devouring eagerly all he saw and writing about it.

In Colombo in Ceylon (now Sri Lanka), he visited the monasteries associated with the Hinayana sect of Buddhists.

On the way to Singapore, he was shown the old haunts of the pirates of the Malay region, whose descendants, as he wrote to an Indian friend, had now taken to peaceful pursuits, for they could not put up resistance against the mightier battleships of the French, British and Dutch that now moved in these seas. At the port of Hong Kong, he saw the many junks and dinghies in the waters and wrote an amusing description of life on a moored boat and how a baby strapped to his mother's back slept soundly on as she moved about carrying loads, jumping with agility from one craft to another, in the midst of boats and steam launches rushing in and out through the waters of one of the busiest port cities in the world.

In a Buddhist monastery at Canton in south-east China, Vivekananda was received with respect as a great saint from India. He saw in China, and later in Japan, many temples with manuscripts written in the ancient Bengali script. This made him realize the extent of India's influence on the world, especially in ancient times. It also strengthened his conviction of the spiritual unity of Asia.

In Japan, he travelled to Yokohama, Osaka, Kyoto and Tokyo. Since the 1880s, Japan had begun to modernize itself after centuries of deliberate isolation. He saw its broad streets, the houses built almost like doll's houses, the pine-covered hills, and the gardens that were intricately designed with shrubs, rockeries, small pools and tiny stone bridges. The innate artistic nature of the Japanese impressed him. On the other hand, the thoroughly organized Japanese army with its impressive armaments made in Japan itself, the country's expanding navy, its merchant ships and factories, revealed to him the scientific skill of a newly awakened Asian nation. He was told that the Japanese regarded India as the 'dreamland of everything noble and great.'

He wrote that he had never seen as patriotic and artistic a people as the Japanese. From Yokohama he crossed the Pacific Ocean and arrived in Vancouver, British Columbia, on the west coast of Canada. Next, he travelled by train to Chicago, where the Parliament of World Religions was scheduled to be held. The lengthiest part of his stay abroad was spent in America, and he travelled to various cities there.

WINNING ACCOLADES IN AMERICA

His impressions of America were mixed: there was admiration and the occasional disillusionment. He thought that Americans had achieved a lot through their hard work, friendly co-operation as well as the application of scientific knowledge.

Chicago was the city he was headed for, since the World Parliament of Religions was convened here. He knew it was the third largest city of America then, after New York and Philadelphia, and it was located by the shore of Lake Michigan. Its teeming population and modern ways of life must have bewildered, excited and terrified the young visitor from India. He was amazed for he knew that not too many years before, Chicago had consisted of only a few fishermen's huts.

He attracted people's notice. Boys ran after him, fascinated by his orange robe and turban, for they were unfamiliar with this kind of attire. The curiosity was not hostile, but in the initial days he found help hard to come by. He found he had reached too early for the Parliament, which was scheduled only for September. It was part of the American exposition to celebrate 400 years of the arrival of the Spanish explorer Christopher Columbus in 1492. In a matter of days Vivekananda found that his money was running out.

He was advised to go to Boston, which was known to be more cosmopolitan, and it was on the train that he made the acquaintance of a kind elderly lady who invited him to be her guest. Then, a professor at Harvard, John Henry Wright, came to his aid and wrote the necessary introductions to the organizers of the Parliament of Religions in Chicago.

Unfortunately, he lost these letters soon after reaching Chicago. As he wandered around Chicago's Lake Shore Drive, tired and exhausted, he sat down by a roadside kerb. A lady at her window noticed him and asked if he had come as a delegate to the Parliament of Religions. He was thus invited into the house of Mr and Mrs George Hale, and it was the beginning of a lifelong friendship between Vivekananda and the Hale family. Later, he carried on a long correspondence with their daughter, Mary.

As the Parliament began, the delegates rose one by one, and read speeches that they had prepared before. Vivekananda had never before addressed such a large assembly. He found himself seized with stage fright, and he requested the chairman, the Reverend Doctor John Henry Barrows, to call him to the stage a little later. This he did a few more times.

At last he came to the rostrum and Dr Barrows introduced him. Bowing to the goddess Sarasvati, the Hindu goddess of wisdom and learning, he turned to address his audience as 'Sisters and Brothers of America.' Instantly, the audience rose to its feet as one and gave him a loud applause. They were moved by his warm words of greeting, so very different from the formal distant tones of the other speakers.

It took a full two minutes before the applause died away, and Vivekananda began his speech by thanking the youngest nation in the world – America in the modern sense had come into being in 1776 after it had declared its independence from the British. The keynote of his address was universal toleration and acceptance. He quoted from Hindu scriptures, revealing their spirit of tolerance, and emphasized that there were different paths all leading to God. In conclusion he pleaded for an end to sectarianism, bigotry and fanaticism.

Vivekananda addressed the Parliament of Religions at least a dozen times more. He presented a paper on Hinduism that delved deep into Hindu metaphysics, psychology and theology. He also spoke of the essential harmony of religions. Vivekananda soon became very popular. From obscurity he leapt to fame. His life-size portraits began appearing in the streets of Chicago, with the words 'The Monk Vivekananda' written underneath. Many onlookers would stop in curiosity, and some chose to express their reverence by bowing their heads.

He was soon much sought after, but as he wrote, fame came with a price. Some overzealous but well-meaning friends, suggested he take elocution lessons, a few others urged him to dress fashionably in order to influence his audiences, and others reprimanded him for mixing with all sorts of people.

NOT JUST AN 'EXOTIC PERFORMER'

After the meetings of the Parliament of Religions were concluded, Vivekananda was invited by a lecture bureau to tour the United States, and he accepted the offer. He wanted money to be free from any obligation to his wealthy friends, and also to help the various philanthropic and religious causes that he had in mind. Further, he thought that through a lecture bureau he could effectively spread his ideas all over America and thus remove from people's minds all false notions regarding Hinduism, and Indian history and culture.

He travelled to cities on the east coast and the mid-west. People soon called him the 'cyclonic Hindu'. He visited, among other places, Iowa, Des Moines, Memphis, Indianapolis, Minneapolis, Detroit, Buffalo, Hartford, Boston, Cambridge, New York, Baltimore and Washington.

However, everything did not always go smoothly. For instance, Vivekananda did not hesitate to criticize anything if he saw it as brutal, inhumane and ignorant. He was irritated by petty questions about India. Soon he discovered that the lecture bureau was exploiting him and he did not like its method of publicity. He began to feel that he was being treated like the chief attraction at a circus. He noticed how its prospectus described his appearance, his height and colour, and even the clothes he wore.

Vivekananda felt disgusted at being treated like an exotic creature in a show and he severed his relationship with the bureau. He now accepted invitations from churches, clubs and private gatherings, and travelled extensively; sometimes he delivered 12 to 14 or even more lectures in a week. People came in large numbers to listen to him, and he met an amazing variety of them, from all walks of life.

WINNING FRIENDS AND INFLUENCING PEOPLE

Vivekananda soon had sincere admirers and devotees among the Americans, who looked after his every comfort, gave him money when he ran out of it, and chose to become his disciples and students. He was particularly grateful to several American women, and in his letters back home he praised them highly. He said they were independent, self-reliant and kind-hearted. They were the 'life and soul of the country' and all learning and culture were centred on them.

His lectures made him popular, and he was offered teaching positions at Columbia and Harvard, established American universities, but he knew he had come to do work of a more enduring nature. Soon after, some poor but earnest students rented some unfurnished rooms in a less affluent section of New York City. He lived in one of these rooms and a room on the second floor of the lodging-house was used for his lectures and classes. Vivekananda sat on the floor when conducting the meetings, while the audience seated themselves around him as best they could, utilizing the marble-topped dresser, the sofa, and even the washstand in the corner. The door was left open and those who came in later filled the hall and sat on the stairs.

The lectures, given every morning and several evenings a week, were free. The rent was paid by voluntary subscriptions raised by students, and the deficit was met by Vivekananda himself with the money he earned from his other lectures on India. Soon the meeting place had to be moved downstairs to occupy an entire floor.

He had spent nearly two years in America and now he was eager to mould the spiritual life of individual students and to train a group that would carry on his work in America in the future. He began to instruct several chosen disciples in Jnana-Yoga in order to clarify for them the subtle truths of Vedanta as found in the Upanishads and the Gita. He also taught them methods of Raja-Yoga that included the science of self-control, concentration and meditation.

He met many interesting people. There was Nikola Tesla, the great scientist who specialized in the field of electricity. In Europe, he would later meet Sir William Thomson (afterwards Lord Kelvin) and Professor Herman von Helmholtz, two leading scientist-philosophers of the time.

He also came in contact with the poor and the humble. There were times he was mistaken for an African-American, but he did not mind. One day, as he alighted from a train in a town where he was to deliver a lecture, an African-

American porter came up to him and said that he had heard how one of his own people had become great and wanted to shake hands with him. Vivekananda shook his hand most warmly and never gave away his true identity. Vivekananda was often refused admittance to a hotel, a barber shop, or a restaurant, because he looked different. When he related these incidents to a shocked disciple, he was asked why he did not tell people that he was not of African-American origin but an Indian and a monk. However, Vivekananda would never seek comfort for himself at the expense of another's humiliation.

Vivekananda made two trips to America. He returned to India from his first visit in January 1897. In between, he also made two trips to Europe.

TRAVELS TO EUROPE

In contrast to his stay in America, Vivekananda's travels to Europe were shorter, but he wrote insightful pieces on his stay and the people he interacted with. His work also garnered success here and this pleased him. He wrote: 'The Americans are quick, but they are somewhat like straw on fire, ready to be extinguished.' He admired the English people, their steadiness, thoroughness, loyalty and perseverance to complete whatever they undertook.

He travelled by the famous Orient Express through Europe. This luxury train ran daily from Paris to Constantinople, and provided excellent facilities to its passengers. It was the year of the Paris Exhibition when he reached the city and the only Indian scientist attending was Sir Jagadish Chandra Bose, who worked on the radio and made important investigations regarding life in plants.

In Paris, Vivekananda willingly showed his hosts and their guests the many ways of wearing a turban and even happily posed for photos. He described the famous theatre actors of the time whom he met in Europe, including Sarah Bernhardt and Emma Calvé.

In Germany, Vivekananda said the Germans were efficient, and the pace of mechanization impressed him as well. He also met celebrated scholars such as Max Müller and Paul Deussen, and spoke of the cultural exchanges that had benefited both countries.

MEMORIES OF HOME IN EUROPE

Vivekananda spent several weeks in Switzerland in the July of 1896, visiting Geneva, Montreux, Zermatt close to the Matterhorn, and Schaffhausen. He felt exhilarated by his long walks in the Alps. He wanted to climb Mont Blanc, but gave up the idea when told of the difficulty of the ascent. He found that Swiss peasant life and the manners and customs of the people were quite similar to the hill people he met when travelling in the Himalayas. In Switzerland, he went mountain climbing and glacial crossing. In a little village at the foot of the Alps, he conceived the idea of founding a monastery in the Himalayas, and he did indeed set up one in Almora, soon after his return to India.

He went on a tour through Vienna, Turkey, Greece and Egypt, and also spent some time in Jerusalem. He described Constantinople, its mosques and streets at great length.

He made observations about Egypt, some of which appeared in a Bengali magazine. Seeing Aden from the ship, one could see only vast stretches of sand and it reminded him of the deserts of Rajasthan he had walked across as a young man. There was a substantial Indian presence in Aden, not just civil and military people but also Parsi shopkeepers and Sindhi merchants.

THE SUEZ AND ITS HISTORY

While sailing on the Suez Canal, Vivekananda wrote a detailed description of sharks in the waters. They kept everyone guessing when they would arrive and a sighting of them caused great excitement.

Vivekananda showed an admirable knowledge of history, and a keen observation of people and their manners. No matter how far he travelled, he was always happy to return home. He often said that the West was the *karma-bhumi*, the land of action, while India was his *punya-bhumi*, the land of holiness. The very dust of India was holy to him.

XIII

INDUMADHAB MALLICK

TRAVELLING EAST

As travelling became more commonplace and easier by the turn of the 20th century, more travel accounts to other places appear. The travelogue of Indumadhab Mallick, a man of many talents, belongs to this category.

He was born in 1869, in Burdwan district of West Bengal. By the time he was twenty-eight, he had completed his post-graduation in subjects as varied as philosophy, physics, botany and zoology. He taught philosophy for a few years in a college in Bengal and later also studied medicine at the Calcutta Medical College. Mallick also wrote erudite articles on science and discoveries of the day in magazines such as the *Modern Review*. He was concerned about various illnesses such as malaria, which in those days had a high mortality rate, and wrote articles stressing the need to develop a vaccine for it.

His book detailing his travels to East Asia, but mainly to China, was written in Bengali and called *Chin Bhramana* (Travels in China). It has detailed and amusing observations, and also tells us of the social and the chaotic political situations in China at that time.

It was the early 20th century, and the Manchu Empire in China was on its way out. A republic was now in place. However, Yuan Shikai, who was China's first president, began to have ambitions of setting up a new dynasty. At the same time, the western powers, encouraged by a militarily weak China had carved out several 'concessions' (settlements) for themselves in China's cities and provinces. Mainly in south and east China, these were ruled as virtually independent territories with little regard to the Chinese government in Peking (now Beijing).

THE CHINESE, EVERYWHERE

Mallick commenced his journey by sea the very year war broke out between Russia and Japan. This was the Russo-Japanese war of 1904, in which the great Russian empire would see a shock defeat at Japan's hands.

Mallick had set out from Calcutta, on a British ship, and its first port of call was Rangoon in Burma (now

Myanmar), then a British territory. The city had Indian traders and labourers, but Mallick was more surprised to see the large presence of several Chinese or 'Chinamen' as he called them, in the city. They were all engaged either in trade or in business. This observation about the presence of Chinese settlers all along East and South-east Asia was confirmed further as he stopped at other places such as Penang in Malaysia, where there were not just Chinese tradespeople and shopkeepers but also labourers.

Mallick was greatly impressed by the hardworking Chinese coolies, who worked skilfully and silently. The scholar of Chinese studies, Narayan Sen, who also translated Mallick's *Chin Bhramana*, describes how Mallick noted the Chinese preference for the colour blue. Blue appeared in most of their clothes. Their small boats, called sampans, in which they plied the narrow waterways whether in Hong Kong or Malaysia, were often painted blue. And most shophouses and even living quarters were painted blue. Even the signboards were done up in blue.

The high-handed and even arrogant behaviour of the Indian policemen in Singapore made Mallick indignant. They had emigrated or had been sent here by the British, for Singapore was a British colony. They did not use merely their sticks to browbeat someone, but they cursed, punched and slapped in equal measure.

As his ship sailed up the South China Sea, Mallick noted that cyclones were frequent in this area, and the months of November and February were especially dangerous. It took a journey of seven days from Singapore before the ship berthed at Hong Kong.

The port had no jetty facilities for passengers wishing to disembark. Instead, they had to take small boats or sampans to go ashore. As soon as a ship neared port, several of these small boats would surround the ship, calling out for passengers. Like Vivekananda before him, Mallick was impressed by the number of women, children strung up on their backs, who rowed these boats. To him, they seemed perfectly content spending days and nights on their boats.

The reflection of their blue and white clothes on the water made a memorable impression on him. He guessed that the boat people had been living this way, in Hong Kong and also in Canton across the Pearl River, for generations and indeed, there seemed to be thousands of them in the waters.

CHINESE CUSTOMS

During his stay in Hong Kong, Mallick acquired a detailed knowledge of certain Chinese customs such as ancestor worship, and their ways of marriage. He also noted the practice of 'foot-binding', which forced young girls to bind their feet tightly, for small feet were a symbol of beauty.

He left Hong Kong for the province of Fujian, where the southern coastal town of Xiamen, then known as Amoy, was located. It took almost five days for Mallick, travelling on another ship, to reach the place from Hong Kong as conditions in the East China Sea and the Formosa Strait (now Taiwan Strait), with its strong winds and huge waves, made travel difficult and slow. It was also after he reached Amoy that he felt he had truly reached China.

The terraced rice fields of Amoy were clearly visible from the ship. Irrigation, he noted, was an especially arduous here. Farmers appeared to be very hard-working, putting in as many as 16 hours of work.

Mallick noted that much of the city of Amoy was extremely dirty. The streets with row houses made of brick on either side, were extremely narrow and filthy. Large pots were placed just by the roadside for people to spit and even relieve themselves right there, and this left a terrible odour all over the place. However, human waste was used as manure. Nothing it seemed, and Mallick noted this with some approval, was wasted in China.

In Amoy, those working with wood made splendid products. They could so easily carve different images on wood with their fine chisel. He brought back with him to India two boxes of artificial flowers so beautiful that they did not seem made by hand.

The nearby island of Gulang (Gulangyu) offered a pleasant change. This was where most of the foreign consulates were located, and it appeared clean and well maintained, in contrast to Amoy. There were gardens, even a well-kept race course, a richly stocked library, hotels and also a theatre that featured entertainments in English and at times German. The people from various countries who lived here had in turn got together to form a 'security association' for their own protection.

The traditional part of Gulang was well known for its temples. Mallick met a priest who knew English, and it was from him that Mallick learnt a bit about the ancient Chinese philosophical systems such as Confucianism and Taoism. Mallick came away with the impression that not just books but even implements of writing such as ink, pens and even paper, were valued in China. Paper that was strewn on streets was collected and taken to temples where it was burnt in an act of piety. The ash, considered auspicious, was in turn collected or given to boatmen or sailors. It was believed that if this ash was tossed into a stormy sea, it would be instantly calmed.

Mallick returned to India by the same route he had taken to Xiamen, but his work does not include any record of his return journey.

Mallick is credited with popularizing the cooking instrument called the 'ICMIC cooker.' The idea for this cooker may have come from his observation of Chinese food vendors. They, as Mallick described, cooked and kept the food warm in round wicker baskets, heaped on top of other, and at the very bottom there was a burning pot filled with charcoal. The vendor carried this contraption on either side of his shoulder pole.

Mallick died fairly young in 1917, when he was only forty-eight.

XIV

BENOY KUMAR SARKAR

WITNESS TO A CHINA IN DECLINE

Benoy Kumar Sarkar was born on 26 December 1887 in Malda, northern Bengal. He was fluent in several languages. He was a teacher of History at the Bengal National College and School that had been set up in 1906, following the nationalist agitation over the British Governor General Lord Curzon's decision to divide Bengal (a decision later revoked in 1911). Later, this institution would become the Jadavpur University. Besides his travel account on China that was written in Bengali and called *'Bartaman Juge Chin Samrajya'* (The Chinese Empire in the Present Age), he wrote other books on China, such as *The Chinese Religion through Hindu Eyes*, which was published in English in 1916.

THE FOREIGNERS IN CHINA

Sarkar reached China in 1915, after having visited Japan and Korea first, though his travel account doesn't mention his visits to these latter two places in detail. His ship anchored at Port Arthur, then in China (present-day Lushunkou and close to North Korea). From here he took a train to the city of Mukden (present-day Shenyang) in north-east China, from where he boarded another train to Peking (Beijing). It was a trip that took almost a day. Peking, he said, reminded him of Cairo, a city he had visited earlier. There was a marked similarity between the two cities in the area known as 'Legation Street', the location of most of the foreign settlements. These, as Mallick had also described, were parts of the city controlled by the foreign powers and called 'concessions.'

Sarkar visited the British concession next to the city of Hankou in Central China. He noted that the rickshaws (pulled by cycle or even hand-drawn) in this area were not allowed entry into the Chinese-inhabited neighbourhoods, just as rickshaws from other parts of the city were barred from the concession areas. The Chinese, thus, had become strangers in their own land. As Mallick had noted in Singapore, Sarkar too described the many Indian soldiers in Hankou working as guards.

HANKOU, A WONDER CITY

Hankou was an important industrial and commercial town. It had China's 'only' iron and steel factory that had been in existence for 20 years and employed about 2,500 people. Several provinces in China were virtually independent, with the centre having no jurisdiction over these. So most traders were required to pay taxes every time they moved into areas controlled by warlords who had become powerful in these provinces and disregarded the central authority in Peking. The very different laws and regulations every province had created confusion and the central treasury received little. It was because the centre at Peking wanted some share of these taxes that it appointed foreign agencies, mainly the British, as tax collectors, but nothing much reached Peking anyway.

Though the situation within the concession areas in Peking and other cities in China bothered Sarkar because these obviously took advantage of the weakness of the Chinese government then, he was deeply impressed by the historical sites he visited. He visited the Lama Temple, the Bell and Drum Tower, the Temple of Heaven and other Confucian temples in Beijing.

THE FORBIDDEN CITY

He described a tour of the Forbidden City, the palace quarter where only the emperor, his family and a large number of dependents once lived. Sarkar saw that some royal rooms were now converted into museums, some functioned as offices, and others had been rented out as hotels. The families of the former Manchu rulers were reduced to living in a small mansion inside the Forbidden City. He also made trips to see the Summer Palace, the tombs of the ancient Ming dynasty, and the Great Wall, which made him get all philosophical.

Sarkar asked in his book if there was really a need to build such a long wall. It had in any case done little to save the country where foreign powers had each carved out rich, beneficial concessions for themselves. The money and manpower (largely farmers) for building the Great Wall could have been well used on building several strong fortresses instead, or even on strengthening the army.

He also provided a detailed analysis of politics in China at the time. The country was heading for serious political trouble and Sarkar proved to be prescient. The new republic gave way to a sham monarchy, and a weakened China soon saw more defeat and humiliation at the hands of the Japanese during the late 1930s and as World War II broke out. By the end of the 1940s, it was the Communists under Mao Zedong who brought the country under their rule and attempt some kind of stability.

Most of his China visit was spent in researching in Shanghai. Before he reached Shanghai, he also travelled to other towns in central China, including Zhengzhou and Luoyang. As he passed through various villages on his way to Luoyang, he spent time at the historic Buddhist temples such as Famous White Horse Monastery and the Shaolin Temple.

CHINA'S WESTWARD GAZE

Sarkar spent about eight months in Shanghai, reading up and researching Chinese history, philosophy and culture. Most of the last section of his book is devoted to Sinology, a detailed look at intellectual life in Shanghai, and includes an appeal to more Indian students to study the Chinese language and the country. He was impressed with the activities of Christian missionaries in China, who had been there for at least two centuries and more, and their contribution to Sinology. He mentions the activities of the Christian Literary Society that had published valuable Chinese texts in English. The city's Saturday Club also organized periodic lectures and programmes attended by people from all walks of life in Shanghai. In the French concession at Shanghai, Sarkar noted a printing press that published books on China, written in French.

The city published a variety of newspapers and magazines in English, French and German languages. There was a monthly journal that dealt with English grammar, literature, spelling and so on, and catered especially to the young Chinese readers who were keen on learning English. Another journal called *Science* reprinted articles originally published in America. These writings were translated with the help of funds and the efforts of Chinese students who were then studying in America. A organization called the World Chinese Students Federation in Shanghai supported the efforts of young Chinese in foreign countries and also provided training to those planning to go abroad. The Federation's founder was Li Denghui, who was a graduate of Yale University. Denghui was also the principal of Fudan College, which in 1917 was renamed Fudan University. An Englishman also instructed students about the Boy Scout movement and a German general imparted military instruction.

In the next 11 years, Sarkar visited several countries in Asia, Europe, Africa and the Americas. During his travels, he gave lectures at reputed universities and institutes, such as at Columbia and Harvard universities in the United States. He even wrote an account of his visit to England in 1925 and called it '*Bilet Bhramana*' (Travels in England). He was a prolific writer and his books – *The Science of History and the Hope of Mankind* and *Introduction to the Science of Education* – were published in London. He died in the US in 1949.

SELECT BIBLIOGRAPHY & FURTHER READING

Abu Taleb Khan, Mirza, *Travels of Mirza Abu Taleb Khan in Asia, Africa, and Europe, during the years 1799, 1800, 1801, 1802, and 1803*, in two volumes, translated by Charles Stewart, Broxbourne, Printed by R. Watts, and sold by Longman, Hurst, Rees, & Orme, 1810, on archive.org.

Burton, Antoinette, *At The Heart of the Empire: Indians and the Colonial Encounter in Late-Victorian Britain*, Berkeley: University of California Press, 1998.

Burton, Antoinette, 'Making a Spectacle of Empire: Indian Travellers in Fin-de-Siecle London', History Workshop, 42 (Fall 1996): 126–46.

Cursetjee, Ardaseer, *Diary of an Overland Journey From Bombay To England, And Of A Year's Residence in Great Britain*, London: Hennington and Galabin, 1840). Also see, http://archiver.rootsweb.ancestry.com/th/read/INDIA/2005-08/ 1125343467.

Dass, Ishuree, A Brief Account of a Voyage to England and America by Ishuree Dass of Futtehgarh, Allahabad: Presbyterian Mission Press, 1851.

Das, Harihar, *Life and Letters of Toru Dutt*, Harihar Das, 1921, OUP, on archive.org.

Das, Harihar, 'Early Indian Visitors to England', Calcutta Review, 3rd series, 13 (1924): 83:114.

Dyer, Helen S., *Pandita Ramabai: The Story of Her Life* (1900) on archive.org.

Emin, Joseph, *Life and Adventures of Joseph Emin, An Armenian,*

Written in English by Himself, London: the Author, 1792; 2nd edition ed. A. Apcar, Calcutta: Asiatic Society of Bengal, 1918.

Fisher, Michael H., *The First Indian Author in English: Dean Mahomed (1759–1851) in India, Ireland, and England*, Oxford University Press, 15 Feb 2000.

Fisher, Michael, *Counterflows to Colonialism: Indian Travellers and Settlers in Britain, 1600–1857*, New Delhi: Permanent Black, 2004.

I'tesamuddin, Mirza Sheikh, *Shigurf Namah-i-Velaet* ed James Edward Alexander and Munshi Shumsher Khan, London, Parbury, Allen, 1827.

I'tesamuddin, Mirza Sheikh, *The Wonders of Vilayet: Being the Memoir, Originally in Persian, of a Visit to France and Britain In 1765*, translated by Kaiser Haq (Translator), Peepul Tree Press, 2002.

Khair, Tabish, Justin Edwards, Martin Leer, Hanna Ziadeh, *Other Routes: 1500 Years of African and Asian Travel Writing*, Bloomington: Indiana University Press, 2006.

Mahomet, Dean, *The Travels of Dean Mahomet, a Native of Patna in Bengal, Through Several Parts of India, While in the Service of the Honourable the East India Company. Written by Himself, in a Series of Letters to a Friend*, in two volumes, Gale Ecco Print Editions, 2010, UK.

Mahomet, Dean, *The Travels of Dean Mahomet: An Eighteenth-Century Journey Through India*, Edited with an introduction and biographical essay by Michael H. Fisher, University of California Press, Berkeley, 1997.

King, Caroline Howard, *In My Time at Salem*, Vermont: Stephen Daye Press, 1937.

Kosambi, Meera, *Pandita Ramabai Through Her Own Words: Selected Works* (translated, edited and compiled) New Delhi: Oxford University Press, 2000.

Lahiri, Shompa, *Indians in Britain: Anglo Indian Encounters: Race and Identity, 1880–1930*, London: Frank Cass, 2000.

Malabari, Behramji M., *The Indian Eye on English Life, or, Rambles of a Pilgrim Reformer*, Bombay, Apollo Printing Works, 1891, accessed on archive.org.

Nowrojee, Jehangeer and Hirjeebhoy Merwanjee, *Journal of a Residence of Two and a Half Years in Britain*, London, W.H. Allen, 1841, accessed on archive.org.

Pandita Ramabai, *Pandita Ramabai's American Encounter: The Peoples of the United States (1889)*, translated and edited by Meera Kosambi, Bloomington: Indiana University Press, 2003.

Sarkar, Benoy Kumar (1916) *Chinese Religion Through Hindu Eyes: a study in the tendencies of Asiatic mentality*, Commercial Press, Shanghai, accessed on archive.org.

Sen, Narayan, 'China as Viewed by Two Early Bengali Travellers', http://indiachinainstitute.org/wp-content/uploads/2009/07/sen-narayan-china-as-viewed-by-two-early-bengali-travellers.pdf.

Sorabji, Cornelia, *India Calling – The Memories of Cornelia Sorabji, India's first woman barrister*, edited Chandani Lokuge, OUP, 2001, also at https://archive.org/details/MemoriesCorneliaSorabji.

Sorabji, Richard, *Opening Doors: The Untold Story of Cornelia Sorabji*, London, I.B. Tauris, 2010.

Sen, Simonti: *Self and Other in Bengali Travel Narratives, 1870–1910*, Orient Longman, 2005.

Southerden, Blair and Helen Clifford, *Ardaseer Cursetjee*, http://blogs.ucl.ac.uk/eicah/files/2014/05/Cursetjee-Final-PDF-19.08.14.pdf.

Visram, Rozina, *Ayahs, Lascars and Princes: Indians in Britain 1700–1947*, Pluto Press, 1984.